Khajuraho

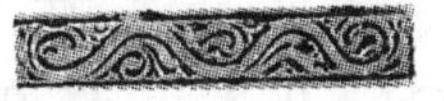

Monumental Legacy

KHAJURAHO

Devangana Desai

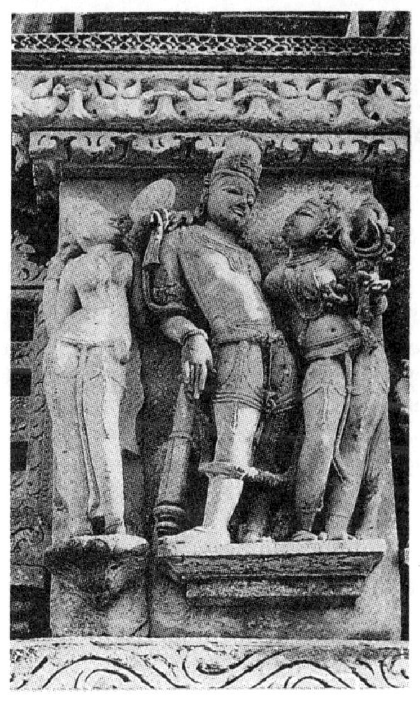

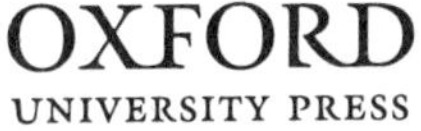

OXFORD
UNIVERSITY PRESS

OXFORD
UNIVERSITY PRESS

YMCA Library Building, Jai Singh Road, New Delhi 110 001

Oxford University Press is a department of the University of Oxford. It furthers the
University's objective of excellence in research, scholarship, and education
by publishing worldwide in

Oxford   New York
Auckland   Bangkok   Buenos Aires   Cape Town   Chennai
Dar es Salaam   Delhi   Hong Kong   Istanbul   Karachi   Kolkata
Kuala Lumpur   Madrid   Melbourne   Mexico City   Mumbai   Nairobi
São Paulo   Shanghai   Taipei   Tokyo   Toronto

Oxford is a registered trade mark of Oxford University Press
in the UK and in certain other countries

Published in India
By Oxford University Press, New Delhi

© Oxford University Press, 2000

The moral rights of the author have been asserted
Database right Oxford University Press (maker)

First Published 2000
Oxford India Paperbacks 2001
Fifth impression 2004

ISBN 0 19 565643 1

Typeset in Goudy
By Eleven Arts, New Delhi
Printed in India at Pauls Press, New Delhi 110 020
Published by Manzar Khan, Oxford University Press
YMCA Library Building, Jai Singh Road, New Delhi 110 001

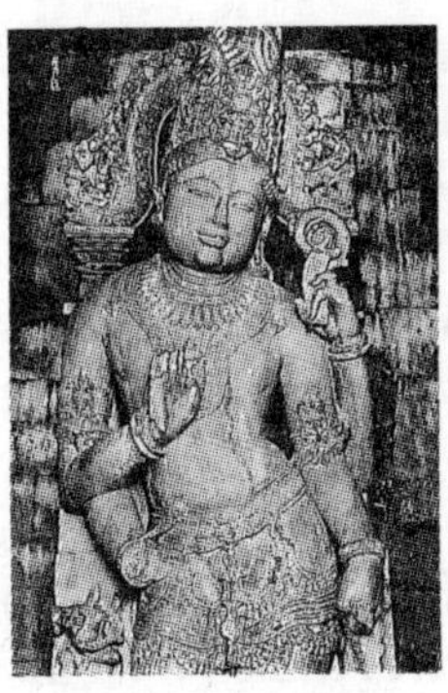

Series Editor's Preface

There are 630 sites on the World Heritage list, as on December 1999, 'inscribed' as properties by the World Heritage Committee of UNESCO. These sites are 'considered to be of outstanding value to humanity', and the preservation of this shared heritage concerns all of us. India has been an active member-state on the World Heritage Forum since 1977, and is one of the countries on the list, with 22 World Heritage Sites. Of these, 17 are recorded as cultural sites, while the rest are natural sites.

I am delighted that the Oxford University Press is publishing brief books on each of the 17 cultural sites, under its series titled *Monumental Legacy*. So far, the following cultural sites in India have been listed as World Heritage sites:

Ajanta Caves (1983), Ellora Caves (1983), Agra Fort (1983), Taj Mahal (1983), Sun Temple, Konarak (1984), Group of Monuments at Mahabalipuram (1985), Churches and Convents of Goa (1986), Group of Monuments at Khajuraho (1986), Group of Monuments at Hampi (1986), Fatehpur Sikri (1986), Group of Monuments of Pattadakal (1987), Elephanta Caves (1987), Brihadisvara Temple, Thanjavur (1987), Buddhist Monuments at

Sanchi (1989), Humayun's Tomb (1993), Qutb Minar and its Monuments (1993), and the Darjeeling Himalayan Railway (1999).

There is scope, indeed, for recognition of many more Indian sites in future on the World Heritage list. I am sure that as, and when, these are declared as World Heritage Sites, they will be included under the Monumental Legacy Series of the Oxford University Press.

The Oxford University Press, in consultation with me, have invited experts in the field to contribute small books, addressed to general readers, on each of these 17 World Heritage Sites in India. These books obviously differ from cheap tourist books and glossy guide books and, at the same time, also from specialized monographs. Their importance lies in the fact they are written by authorities on the subject, to enable visitors to see the monuments in proper perspective.

My sincere thanks to all the authors of the Series and to the editorial staff at the OUP. Bela Malik, Commissioning Editor, History and Ecology, OUP, has been the main sustaining force and has shared the joys and excitements since the initiation of the Series. To her, and Sourav Dutta, Assistant Editor, I am most grateful for their constant support and enthusiasm in the project.

March 2000   D.D.

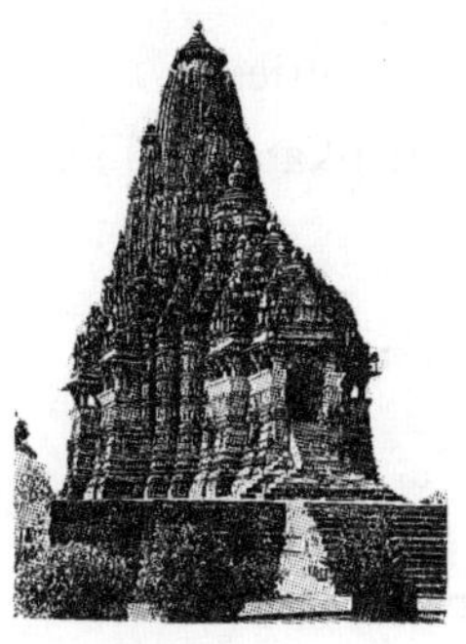

Contents

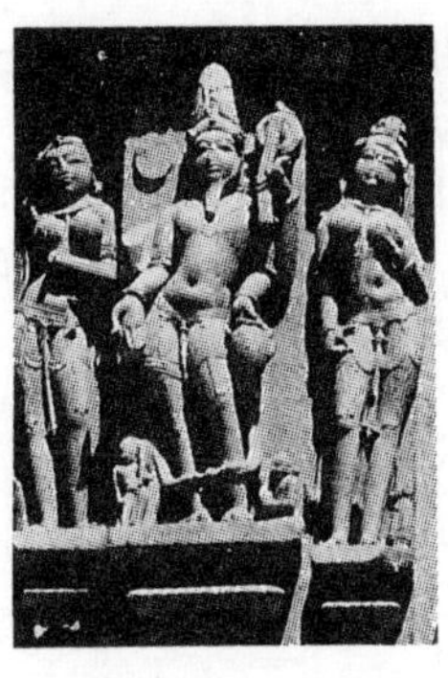

List of Illustrations

Maps

Figs.

Photographs

Black and White:

Colour:

Cover Photo: Celestial maiden, Vishvanatha temple, Khajuraho

Acknowledgements for permission to reproduce Drawings (Figures):

Archaeological Survey of India: Figs. II, X, XI; The British Library, London: Fig. I; Franco-Indian Research, Mumbai: Figs. III–V, VII–IX, XII

Photograph Credits:

American Institute of Indian Studies: 2–5, 7, 11–13, 15, 17–20, 22, 24, 25; Archaeological Survey of India: 1; Carmel Berkson: Cover photo, 6, 8, 10, 21; Devangana Desai: Colour photo C; Franco-Indian Research: Colour photos A, B, D; Chandrakant Kothari: 14, 23; Dileep Purohit: 9, 16

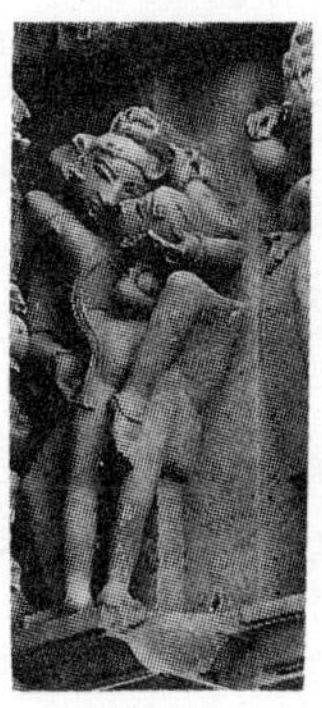

Preface and Acknowledgements

I first visited Khajuraho in 1963. At that time, there were no hotels in this remote village. Only the Circuit House provided some basic accommodation. Today, the village has developed as a major tourist centre with at least five 5-star hotels and many other comfortable lodging places. Khajuraho is connected to several Indian cities through daily air services and road transport. It is part of the tourist itinerary along with Agra (Taj) and Benaras. But despite the tourist traffic, I am happy to say that the place still retains an atmosphere of peace and calm. Khajuraho preserves the ambience of a village and at the same time offers the most modern facilities to visitors. It is a wonderful place where one can have the best of both worlds— ancient and modern.

Erotic sculpture is not the only attraction of Khajuraho. Its temples are among the greatest monuments of medieval India. This marvellous site, particularly the western group of temples, was recognized as a World Heritage site by the UNESCO in 1986. Adding to the attraction of these monuments, there are several historical and natural sites of great scenic beauty in the vicinity of Khajuraho.

As the world celebrates its millennium, Khajuraho's Vishvanatha Temple, consecrated in AD 999, also completed 1000 years of existence. The Government of India and the State of Madhya Pradesh earmarked March 1999–March 2000 as the Millennium Year of Khajuraho. We may note, however, that the antiquity of the site goes beyond a millennium. The Archaeological Survey of India has identified eighteen mounds that are even older and has begun excavation at some of them.

*

I record my gratitude to the Director General, Archaeological Survey of India, and the Director, the American Institute of Indian Studies, Gurgaon, for supplying photographs as listed under Photograph Credits, and for permitting me to reproduce drawings, as mentioned under the list of Figures.

I sincerely thank M. Postel and Dr. Kirit Mankodi of Franco-Indian Research, Mumbai, for giving me permission to reproduce some of the drawings from *The Religious Imagery of Khajuraho*, published by them under the Project for Indian Cultural Studies. I also thank them for the three colour photographs as listed under credits.

To Tulsi Vatsal, I owe a special word of thanks for editing the typescript and making valuable suggestions.

I am grateful to Carmel Berkson, Chandrakant Kothari, and Dileep Purohit for kindly lending me photographs from their collections for the book. I thank Sheril Castelino and Aniruddha Kudalkar for preparing the maps.

I am beholden to the people of Khajuraho, the ASI staff and the ITDC (Ashok) staff, who make me feel at home in Khajuraho.

To Jayant Desai, my husband, I am indebted for his constant encouragement and support throughout my research work and writings.

I am grateful to Oxford University Press, and Bela Malik, Commissioning Editor, History and Ecology, for giving me this opportunity to write on my favourite subject in this *Monumental Legacy* series. I also thank Sourav Dutta and the editorial staff for their meticulous work.

Above all, this book is dedicated to the gods and goddesses who inhabit the temples of Khajuraho.

Mumbai   Devangana Desai

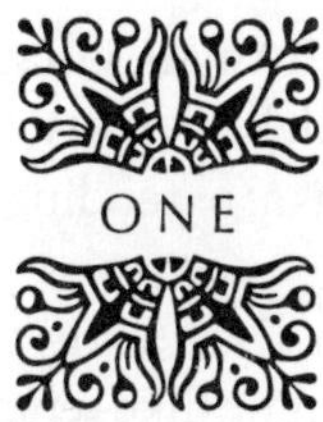

ONE

Introduction

One of the most extraordinary archaeological sites in India, Khajuraho (latitude: 24°51' north, longitude: 79°56' east) in Chhatarpur district of Madhya Pradesh, preserves the country's largest and most magnificent groups of medieval temples. It is located on the banks of the Khudar Nala, a tributary of the Ken river (ancient Karnavati). The area is surrounded by scenic waterfalls, and the low-lying hills of the Vindhya range, locally called Datla

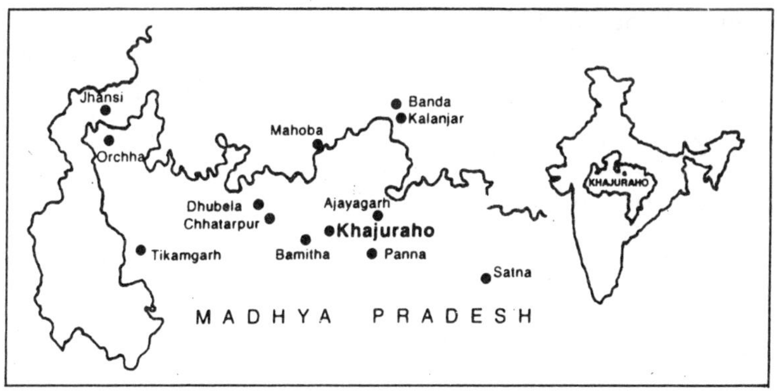

Khajuraho, Madhya Pradesh

and Lavania Pahads, which provide a lovely backdrop to the temple complex. Khajuraho is situated 49 km east of Chhatarpur, 44 km north-west of Panna, 65 km south of Mahoba and 175 km south-east of Jhansi.

Today, Khajuraho is a small village. But between AD 900 and 1200, under the Chandella dynasty, it was a flourishing temple town, called Kharjuravahaka, extending over an area of 13 square kilometres.

The first impression that a visitor gets of Khajuraho is overwhelming: Huge mountain-like temples, free-standing in open space, each square inch covered with sculptures. On coming closer, greeted by whistling birds and parrots, one enters a medieval world inhabited by gods and goddesses, celestial maidens (*apsaras, surasundaris*), mythical animals (*vyalas, makaras*), warriors, dancers, and musicians, all carved on the temple walls. Each temple is a monumental three-dimensional sculpture in itself.

A tradition records that once there were eighty-five temples in Khajuraho; but now only twenty-five remain in varied states of preservation. They stand picturesquely on the banks of lakes, amidst agricultural fields and gardens. The temples and the water tanks are the main monuments at Khajuraho. Except for a couple of them, the temples are not used for worship today, though they were originally built for this purpose.

But why so many temples? Who built them? What gods do they enshrine? What are the erotic sculptures and sensuous female figures doing on their walls? Were these the temples of the *Kamasutra?* Was there free love at this place? These are some questions that come to mind when one visits Khajuraho.

The antiquity of the site has been traced back to prehistoric times, as artefacts belonging to the Middle and late Stone Age and Neolithic industries have been unearthed here. But there is no evidence of the township of Khajuraho prior to AD 900. The building of the temples at Khajuraho began from AD 900 onwards, when local chieftains of the Chandella family amassed power and wealth and rose to be a major political dynasty in northern India.

The region of Madhya Pradesh where Khajuraho is situated is rich in artistic traditions. Maurya remains from the fourth century

BC have been found at Datia in the vicinity of Khajuraho. In the second century BC, the region reverberated with the sound of Buddhist pilgrims at Bharhut and Sanchi (another World Heritage Site). Under the Gupta and Vakataka rulers, in the fifth and sixth centuries AD, Hindu temples, adorned with exquisite sculptures, were constructed at Devgadh, Bhumara, Nachna, Khoh, Eran, and other nearby sites. In the ninth century, under the Pratihara dynasty, several temples were erected, of which one may mention the Mother goddess (Jarai Mata) temple at Barwasagar near Jhansi, the Sun temple at Mankhera near Tikamgadh, and the temples at Mau-Suhania and Kainri in Chhatarpur district. Even at Khajuraho, the influence of the Pratihara style can be seen in the recently excavated sculptures from the north-eastern region of the site.

Travellers' Accounts

Muslim travellers of the medieval period have left some interesting accounts of Khajuraho. The historian Alberuni, who accompanied Mahmud of Ghazni during his raids on central India in AD 1022, mentions 'Kajuraha' as the capital town of Jejahuti (Jejakabhukti), the region ruled by the Chandellas. The place continued as an important religious centre until the fourteenth century, even after the power of the Chandellas had declined. In AD 1335, the Arab traveller Ibn Battuta visited Khajuraho to witness the 'Jogis' (mendicants) and their magic. In his memoirs, he describes a large pond, one mile in length, surrounded by tall temples. This must be the Shivsagara tank near the western group of temples.

By the sixteenth century, however, Khajuraho had vanished into oblivion. It is not even mentioned in Mughal records, although the *Ain-i-Akbari* describes the nearby fort-town of Kalanjar, including the huge Bhairava image outside the Nilakantheshvara temple. It seems that a jungle had engulfed the site of Khajuraho by this time.

Re-emergence in the Nineteenth Century

Gradually in the nineteenth century, Khajuraho re-emerged in the world of art and history. On 3 February 1813, Lieutenant William Price presented a paper at the Asiatic Society of Bengal on the subject of a Sanskrit inscription found at Mau near Khajuraho, which for the first time drew the attention of historians to the royal family of the Chandella dynasty. In 1818, Khajuraho (Kajrow) found a place on the map prepared by Franklin.

Captain T. S. Burt, a British engineer, visited Khajuraho on a day's trip from Chhatarpur in 1838 and published a colourful account of the western group of temples in the *Journal of the Asiatic Society of Bengal* (Vol. VIII), which attracted the notice of art lovers and antiquarians. Burt also took an impression of King Dhanga's inscription, (now in the Vishvanatha temple). Recognizing the importance of these temples, this first British visitor wrote: '... before finally taking the leave of the seven temples, I shall state my opinion, that they are most probably the finest aggregate number of temples congregated in one place to be met with in all India, and all are within a stone's throw of one another.'

Between 1843 and 1847, Maharaja Pratap Singh of Chhatarpur carried out extensive repair work on the Khajuraho temples. He was the first local ruler to take keen interest in their conservation. In his enthusiasm, however, he used lime and brick in the repair work, and this ill-suited the ancient monuments. Some of these renovations were later removed by the Archaeological Survey.

The earliest drawings of Khajuraho were made in 1852 by General F. C. Maisey [**Fig. I**]. These are preserved in the India Office Library, London. Incidentally, Maisey has extensively described the antiquities of the Chandella fort site of Kalanjar as well, along with numerous drawings.

A more systematic description of Khajuraho was given by Major Alexander Cunningham, who visited the place first in 1852 and later in 1864–65 as the Archaeological Surveyor to the Government of India. His accounts in *The Archaeolgical Survey of India Reports*, Volumes II, VII, X, and XXI, are a rich source of information on this site. He recognized its importance and declared that the area contains 'perhaps the largest group of costly Hindu temples that is now to be found in Northern India'.

Raja Deen Dayal was among the first to photograph the Khajuraho temples in 1882. His photographs were published in L. Griffin's *Famous Monuments of Central India* in 1886. In 1892,

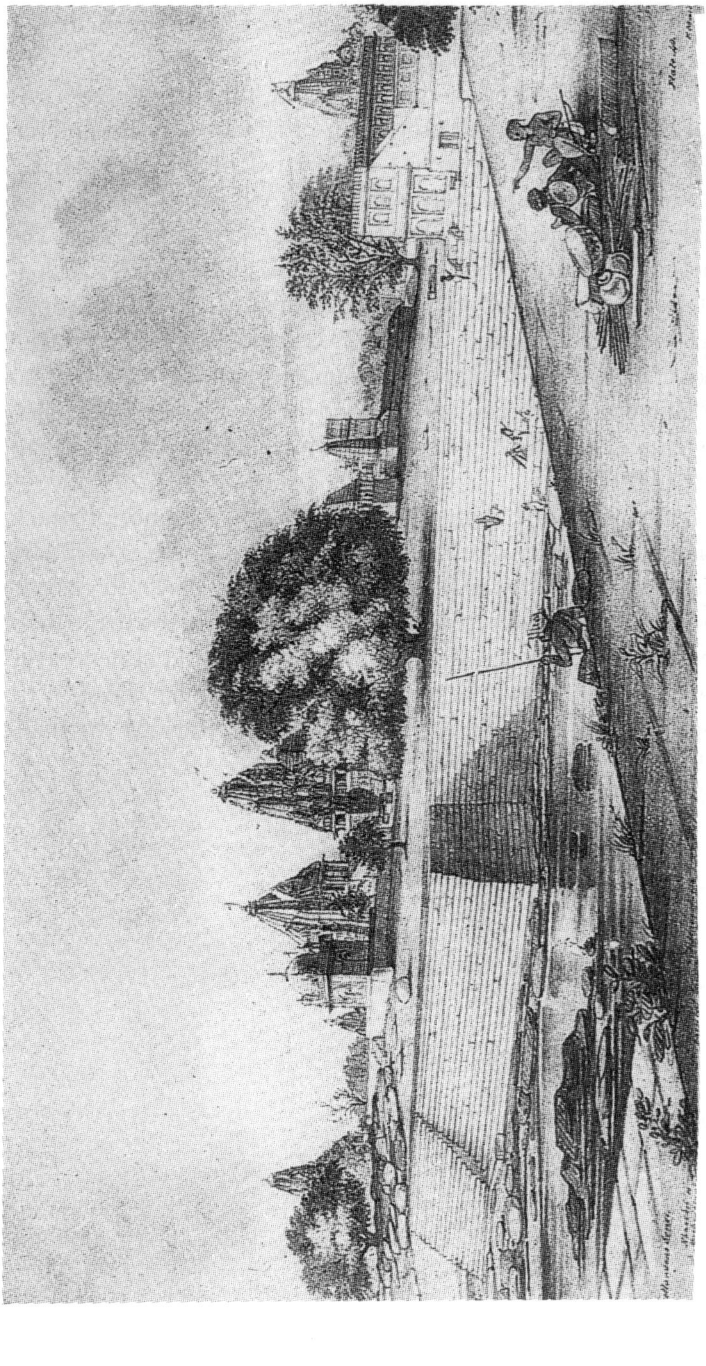

Fig. 1. The earliest drawing of the Khajuraho temples, prepared by F.C. Maisey in 1852

F. Kielhorn published some major inscriptions of Khajuraho in the first volume of the *Epigraphia Indica*.

In 1904, the Archaeological Survey of India introduced a systematic conservation and protection programme for Khajuraho, under the plan drawn up by Sir John Marshall and Henry Cousens. The repair and conservation work of the temples is described by Krishna Deva, the former Director of the ASI, in his book, *The Temples of Khajuraho*, Vol. I, pp.12–14. Some of the temples, such as the Chaturbhuja, Duladeva, Devi Jagadamba, and the Chitragupta, were extensively repaired. From 1953 onwards, the ASI has taken direct charge of the Khajuraho monuments and there is an intensive campaign for the conservation and preservation of the temples. The temples and the Archaeological Museum are under the supervision of the ASI.

There are more than fifty mounds at Khajuraho, of which eighteen have been identified by the ASI for future excavation. Recently, a finely carved plinth of a large early-eleventh century temple has been uncovered in the southern area of the site, not far from the airport. This indicates the archaeological richness of the area, its potential yet to be further revealed, although the majestic temples already proclaim the greatness and importance of the place.

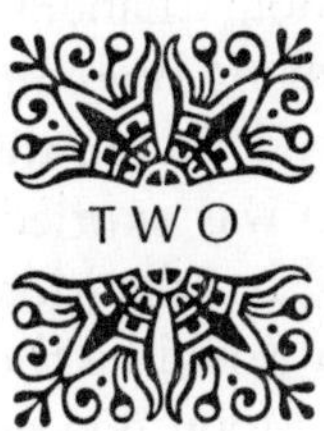

T W O

Patrons—The Chandella Royal Family

The Khajuraho temples were built over a period of 250 years (c. AD 900–1150) during the rule of the Chandella dynasty—either by the rulers themselves or by their chiefs and Jain merchants. The Chandellas were originally local chieftains, who recognized the supremacy of the imperial Pratihara monarchs of Kanauj. Soon, however, the region acquired the name 'Jejakabhukti', after the chief Jeja, or Jayashakti, third in the list of the Chandella genealogy (see Appendix 2), and gradually, by the middle of the tenth century, the Chandella family became independent, and stopped recognizing the overlordship of the Pratihara kings. It was in this period, when the local chieftains of the Khajuraho region became established as a northern Indian power, that this site acquired importance.

The frontiers of this Chandella kingdom, Jejakabhukti, varied from time to time but the area roughly corresponded to what is now known as Bundelkhand. At the height of Chandella power in the eleventh century, this territory was bounded on all four sides by rivers: on the north lay the Yamuna, on the south the

Narmada, on the east the Tamasa (Tons), and on the west the Chambal.

A local Bundelkhandi legend romantically traces the descent of the Chandellas directly from Chandra, the Moon god. According to the story, a beautiful young Brahmin maiden, Hemavati, had an affair with the Moon god. Out of this relationship was born a handsome boy. Hemavati was worried about the future of the child born out of wedlock, but the Moon god comforted her and prophesied that their son would be the first king of Khajuraho. When he grows up, the Moon god added, he should perform *Bhandya Yajna*, a sacrificial ritual that included among its rites the depiction of erotic figures. He should also build eighty-five temples at Khajuraho, carved with erotic figures. This would free his mother from the blemish of extramarital love.

This is how a seventeenth century legend attempts to account for the large number of temples and their erotic sculptures. The legend also accounts for the mythic origin of the Chandella family.

More than sixty-five inscriptions of the Chandellas, who ruled over Jejakabhukti (Bundelkhand) from *circa* AD 831 to 1308, have been found. The inscriptions are, however, silent about this love story. They trace the descent of the Chandellas from the mythic sage Chandratreya (See Appendix Two). The efforts of the Chandella rulers to glorify the origin of their dynasty in inscriptions is noteworthy in the context of the family's possible tribal associations. Their connection with the tribal Gonds and Bhars has been suggested by many historians, as they worshipped a tribal deity called Maniya Devi, and had family ties with the Gonds. Like other Rajput families, the Chandellas further tried to legitimize their social status by building temples, tanks, and by giving gifts to priestly Brahmins. Temple building was emphasized in the medieval Puranas as an important religious practice that brought fame and merit to the builder [**Ph.1**]. Apart from Khajuraho, the Chandellas also built temples and water tanks at Mahoba, Dudhahi, Devgadh, Madanpur, Kalanjar, and Ajaygadh. The last two places were fort towns of strategic importance [**See Chapter VIII, Around Khajuraho**].

Khajuraho was definitely considered a special site and this is

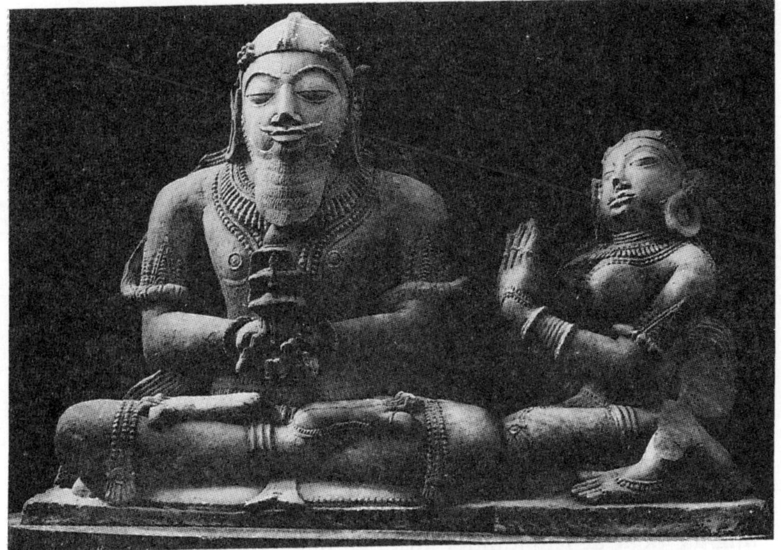

Photo 1. Chandella king and queen performing a ritual, ASI Museum

where the Chandellas concentrated their temple-building activity. Their earlier temples, built when they were still local feudatories, were made of rough granite and constructed on the periphery of the site. Among these are the Chausath Yogini sanctuary for the worship of the Sixty-four Yoginis (goddesses) and the Shiva temple, called Lalguan Mahadeva.

A newly-emerging prince of the dynasty, **Harshadeva** (c. AD 905–925), sixth in the line, successfully fought the Rashtrakuta king, who was the foe of his overlord, and reinstated the Pratihara ruler Kshitipaladeva on the throne of Kanauj in AD 917. This victorious event has been recorded in a stone inscription found near the Vamana temple at Khajuraho. Harsha's marriage with the Rajput princess Kanchuka of the Chahamana family indicates the rise in his social status. With this Chandella ruler can be associated the recently excavated brick complex in the northeastern area of the site, and the 'Brahma' temple on the bank of the Khajursagar lake.

It was Harshadeva's son, **Yashovarman** (c. AD 925–950), who really established the Chandellas as an independent power.

Yashovarman acquired the prestigious Vaikuntha-Vishnu image from his Pratihara overlord Devapala, and announced his victory by building a splendid temple, the first in the Nagara style at Khajuraho, adorning it profusely with sculptures. It is now known as the Lakshmana temple. The temple is made of finely grained sandstone brought from the quarries near Panna, not far from Khajuraho. The inscription on the Lakshmana temple declares Yashovarman's conquest of the strategic fort of Kalanjar. It was from his time that the Chandella king began calling himself 'Lord of Kalanjar'. The king also installed a huge icon of the Boar (Varaha), the third incarnation of Vishnu, in front of the Lakshmana temple. The Boar, who in Hindu mythology rescued the Earth Goddess from the primeval waters, had become a political metaphor in India by the fifth century AD, and symbolized the king saving the earth by vanquishing enemies. By installing the mighty Boar at Khajuraho, Yashovarman asserted his own regal power.

King **Dhangadeva** (c. AD 950–999), his son, expanded the kingdom and ruled over a vast tract stretching between the Yamuna and Narmada rivers. He was the first independent Chandella ruler who refused to acknowledge the suzerainty of the Pratiharas. He was a worshipper of Shiva and installed two *lingas*, one made of emerald and the other of stone, in the temple then called Marakateshvara (Lord of Emerald), and now known as the Vishvanatha temple. The temple was consecrated in AD 999, after Dhangadeva's death.

King **Vidyadhara** (c. AD 1003–1035), Dhangadeva's grandson, is described as the most powerful Indian ruler of his time by the contemporary Muslim chronicler, Ibnul-Athir. Vidyadhara played an important role in mobilizing the Indian princes against the raids of Mahmud of Ghazni. To celebrate his victory, he built the grandest temple at Khajuraho, the Kandariya Mahadeva.

Vidyadhara's successors **Vijayapala** (c. AD 1035–1050) and **Devavarman** (c. AD 1050–1060) lost part of their territory to their powerful neighbours. It was king **Kirtivarman** (c. AD 1060–1100), who reestablished Chandella authority after defeating the neighbouring Chedi ruler of the Jabalpur region. He celebrated his victory by staging an allegorical play *Prabodhachandrodaya*, written by the court poet Krishna Mishra. Significantly, the play ridicules extreme Tantric sects such as the Kapalikas. The king built temples at Mahoba, Kalanjar, and Ajaygadh, and the first Chandella coins were issued in his reign.

The next ruler of note, **Jayavarman** (*c.* AD 1110–1120), carried out some renovation work at Khajuraho and possibly built the Chaturbhuja temple, with its exquisite Vishnu (Narayana) image. He is described in an inscription as a devotee of Narayana. With King **Madanavarman** (*c.* AD 1128–1165), the last great Chandella ruler, can be associated the Duladeva temple, the last lofty monument at Khajuraho. **Parmardideva** (*c.* AD 1165–1203), grandson of Madanavarman, was a patron of poets and a scholar. His enmity with the powerful Rajput king Prithiviraja Chauhan has been recorded in the bardic annals of the *Prithiviraj Raso* and the *Paramal Raso*. He was defeated by Qutbuddin Aibak in 1202, following which the power of the Chandellas, like that of several other Rajput dynasties in northern India, declined in the thirteenth century.

The prosperity and flourishing of Khajuraho as a temple town was closely associated with the rise and strength of the Chandella family, and of the sophisticated culture that flourished under their patronage. The Chandella kings not only commissioned temples and tanks, they also encouraged literature, dance, and music. King Dhangadeva was praised in inscriptions for his learning and for his discernment of the arts. Gandadeva and Paramardideva were themselves poets. Paramardi composed a Sanskrit poem on Shiva and Parvati, which was inscribed on the Nilakantheshvara temple at Kalanjar in AD 1201. The court poets of the Chandellas composed plays, in Sanskrit, which were staged at *yatras* or religious festivals. Knowledge of Sanskrit language and grammar was highly appreciated by the elite. It is this Sanskritized and refined culture that is reflected in the visual arts of the Khajuraho temples.

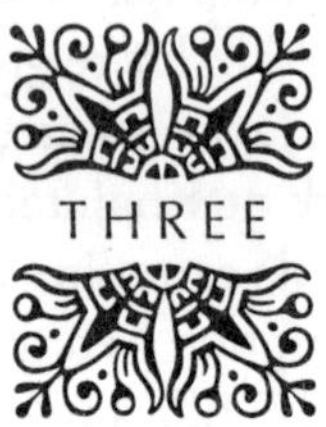

THREE

Religious Background

Sometimes people ask whether there was any religion at all in Khajuraho? There is a generally-held belief that 'free love' abounded there. For many, the name Khajuraho is synonymous with erotic sculpture. Nothing is further from the truth. Erotic figures consist of not even one-tenth of the total number of sculptures that adorn the walls of the temples at Khajuraho. There are hundreds of images of divinities, many holding manuscripts and several in yogic postures. Khajuraho was not a royal playground, but a place of worship and religious discourse, where many sects received patronage. It is also important to bear in mind that the monuments at Khajuraho were religious structures, temples, built by their patrons for worship and for acquiring merit (*punya*) and fame. Temples were the centres of both religious and artistic expression in medieval India.

The tutelary deity of the Chandellas was Maniya Devi, a tribal goddess, whose shrines are simple structures. These are found at Mahoba and Maniyagadh (Rajgadh) on the left bank of the Ken river. In the nineteenth century, Beglar, a colleague of Major Cunningham, described this deity as a compromise between the

Brahmanical Parvati and the female deity worshipped by some Gond tribes. A seventeenth-century account attributed to a bard called Chand also mentions Maniya Devi as the family goddess of the Chandellas, to whom they appealed in times of danger.

But the temples built by the Chandellas at Khajuraho are built in the sophisticated Nagara style and affiliated to the Brahmanical or Hindu religion, and those by their ministers and merchants to the Jain Digambara faith. Of the twenty-five temples extant today, ten enshrine Vishnu in his various forms, such as Vamana (the Dwarf), Varaha (the Boar), and Vaikuntha, a composite form. Eight are dedicated to Shiva, one to Surya, one to the Sixty-four Yoginis

> *Religious Affiliation of Khajuraho Temples*
> 10 Vishnu (Vamana, Varaha, Vaikuntha)
> 8 Shiva
> 1 Surya
> 1 Sixty-four Yoginis
> 5 Jain Digambara

(goddesses), and five to the Jain faith. Many more temples were constructed on the site, of which now only epigraphs and sculptures remain. A colossal image of Hanuman with an inscription from AD 922 attests to the worship of the monkey god.

A solitary image of the Buddha was found by Major Cunningham in the eastern area of the site. It bears an inscription of the Buddhist faith, beginning with 'Ye dharma hetu prabhava...', suggesting the prevalence of Buddhism on this site, though on a limited scale. Vajrayana Buddhist images from about the eleventh century (now in the Museum at Lucknow) were also found at the Chandella town of Mahoba, 65 km away. Recent excavations at the Bijamandala mound in the southern area of Khajuraho seem to suggest a Shiva (Vaidyanatha) temple of the early eleventh century. Some Jain images have been excavated along with those of Shiva and Vishnu.

The main group of Jain temples, situated in the eastern area of the site, was patronized by the merchant community, who belonged to the Digambara sect. The temples were dedicated to Tirthankaras Adinatha (Rishabhanatha), Parshvanatha (installed later in 1860), and Shantinatha. A colossal image (4.3 m. or 14 ft high) of Shantinatha has a dedicatory inscription from AD 1027–28. Many images of Tirthankaras were installed by individual donors. Several images of Jain Yakshis and Kshetrapalas have been found in the temples and also as detached sculptures, which are now housed in the museums. On the door jamb of the Parshvanatha temple is incised a magic square with numerals arranged in such a way that their sum in any direction is always thirty-four. This indicates the interest of the Jain community in magic. Some *stambhas* (pillars) bearing Jain divinities are found to the south of the Yogini temple.

Popular belief erroneously associates Khajuraho with the extreme Tantric sect of the Kapalikas, who were Brahmin-haters, who had their food in the skulls of the upper-caste Brahmins, and who, it is believed, indulged in sexual rites. In the literature of the period, the Kapalikas were portrayed as practising gruesome rites, abducting beautiful girls for sacrificing to the Devi, the Goddess. But it does not seem likely that this not-so-organized sect of the Kapalikas could be associated with these meticulously planned temples. D.N. Lorenzen, a leading authority on the history of the Kapalika sect, also dissociates this sect from the Khajuraho temples.

It is important to note that Khajuraho represents a stage in Indian history when orthodox Brahmin forces reasserted themselves against extreme Tantric sects such as the Kapalikas. In the allegorical play *Prabodhachandrodaya*, composed by the Chandella court poet Krishna Mishra, there is a metaphoric animosity between the virtuous King Discrimination (Viveka) and his opponent King Great Delusion (Mahamoha). The anti-Vedic, extreme Tantric sects of the Kapalikas, Kshapanakas (Jain), Vajrayana Buddhists, and Charvakas are portrayed as allies of the Great Delusion, whereas Vishnu-Bhakti (Devotion), Sarasvati and Upanishad (Vedantic Lore) help King Discrimination win his battle against Great Delusion.

The religion at Khajuraho was Tantric-Puranic. It was a composite and mixed religion with both Tantric and Puranic elements. By the tenth century AD, the Puranas, which had earlier opposed the Tantras, now accepted several Tantric elements such as *mantras*, *yantras*, and *mandalas*. At the same time, the inscriptions at Khajuraho support Brahmins and the ancient tradition of the Vedas, extolling the Three Vedas (Trayi). The religious practice of the *Purta-dharma*, which involves *dana* or gift-giving to Brahmins, and building of temples, tanks, and undertaking of charitable works, was strongly recommended in the Puranas. The Chandella king Dhangadeva donated gold and land to the Brahmins. His inscription of AD 999 mentions that he performed a special ceremony called *Tulapurushadana* in which he weighed himself in gold and distributed this gold to Brahmins. The performance of *yajna* (sacrifice to fire) was also glorified in inscriptions. King Vidyadhara's wife Satyabhama made donations on a day of solar eclipse. The Chandellas believed in merits accruing from gift-giving during an eclipse.

The composite religious practices at Khajuraho are exemplified in the Lakshmana, one of the major Vishnu temples that enshrines the esoteric icon of the god Vaikuntha. Built in AD 954, it was associated with Tantric Vaishnavism of the Kashmir school (Pancharatra). The Chandella king Yashovarman had acquired the Vaikuntha image as a war trophy—it had originally come from the Kashmir-Chamba region where the god Vaikuntha was worshipped according to the Pancharatra religion. The Kandariya Mahadeva, one of the grandest of the Khajuraho temples, built in about AD 1030, was affiliated to the moderate Tantric Shaivite order, called Siddhanta.

Both these Tantra-based Vaishnavite and Shaivite orders existed side-by-side and functioned within the Brahmanic fold. Unlike the Kapalika sect, they were not extreme Tantric, but were influenced by the Vedic revival and had incorporated Puranic elements. Both systems believed in the role of Shakti or Female Energy in the Creation and Dissolution of the universe. The Supreme Being (Para-Vasudeva or Para-Shiva) is both transcendent and unmanifest, and also immanent and manifest in graded powers and elements. Theologians bridged the gap between the formless and form by bringing in intermediary stages. In order to become an instrument of meditation and worship, the unmanifest becomes manifest in form through various images. This development led to a hierachical order in images: the principal divinity and its emanations and sub-emanations. The iconic schemes of the temples indicate gradation of images in relation to the the centre (i.e. the principal divinity) of the sanctum. In short, the architects have presented the temple as cosmos.

The feudal socio-economic set-up of the period favoured the construction of large edifices with opulent sculptural decoration. The corresponding developments in the techniques of architecture made it possible to visibly render the multitude of images. Numerous projections and indentations on the temple design helped to accommodate a vast pantheon. This applies to most of the temples of Khajuraho, whether dedicated to Vishnu, Shiva, Surya, or Jain Tirthankaras.

The central purpose of religion—the attainment of the ultimate reality—is expressed by presenting the temple as cosmos. This is the internal logic of the iconic imagery of the temple, articulated while the designer was conscious of the central purpose of religion. This does not, however, imply that the Khajuraho patrons were esoteric. Visitors to the temples, and pilgrims, need not be aware of the philosophies underlying the imagery.

People from all walks of life visited the temples. Religious aspirants as well as common people with mundane desires would worship according to their level of understanding and faith. But the temple served as more than just a place of worship. It was a socio-religious institution in the medieval period, as it is today. In the halls of temples, religious texts were recited, and dance and music was performed. The Chandella dramatists composed plays, both mythical and farcical, to be staged during temple festivals (yatras). People even came to Khajuraho in search of magical cures for diseases, as is indicated in the inscription at the Vaidyanatha temple and in the colourful account of Ibn Battuta.

With numerous temples dedicated to various divinities, Khajuraho was an active religious centre. One can imagine the bustling religious and artistic activities, with several priests conducting worship in different temples; royal priests supervising the construction of temples, as in the case of Dhangadeva's Vishvanatha temple; and royal preceptors like Acharya Urdhvashiva guiding the philosophy and rituals of religious systems. Patrons like King Dhangadeva and Gahapati Kokkala invited groups of Brahmins, well-versed in the Vedas, to settle near the Shiva temples built by them. There were dancing girls like Mahanachani Padmavati (mentioned in the Kalanjar inscription), who performed and also donated to the temples. There were architects and their team of masons and sculptors, musicians, dance teachers, as well as traders, as depicted in the numerous sculptural panels of the Khajuraho temples. All this clearly indicates that Khajuraho was an active religious and cultural centre in the medieval period.

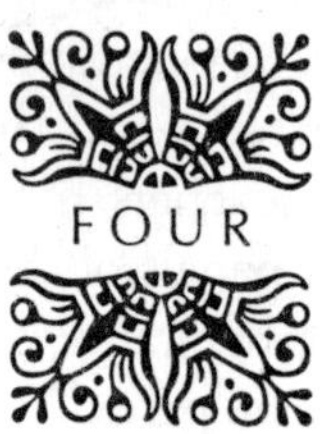

FOUR

Temple Architecture:
Concept and Stylistic Features

Main Features

The Khajuraho temples are built in the central Indian Nagara style of architecture. In this style, the spire (*shikhara*) is curvilinear in form. Although the temples are affiliated to different religious sects—Hindu and Jain—they have a cognate architectural style. They are unified structures consisting of four or five units: a cella or sanctum (*garbhagriha*), a vestibule (*antarala*), a large hall (*mahamandapa*), another hall (*mandapa*), and a porch (*mukhamandapa*) [**Ph. 2, Fig. II**]. Most of the Khajuraho temples are erected on the east-west axis and therefore face the direct rays of the rising sun.

The garbhagriha, literally 'womb chamber', is the name given to the innermost sanctum in an Indian temple. The temple is conceived of as an abode of god, whose emblem or icon is installed in this innermost chamber. The sanctum is a dark, peaceful place, where the devotee is reborn to higher life. It is a hollow chamber resembling a cave (*guha*) and its centre is considered to be the centre of the universe. The temple's spire rises exactly above the centre of the sanctum. The invisible axis joining the centre of the sanctum on the ground level and the finial of the superstructure above is conceived as the Cosmic Axis connecting earth and heaven.

The earlier temples in India, built in the fifth century AD, generally consisted of only the sanctum and an attached porch. Gradually, with changing requirements for rituals, more structures were added to this simple scheme. A hall for dance performances and another for food offerings to the deity were added and the original two-unit scheme was expanded to have four or five units.

The Indian temple is built according to the canons laid down in the texts called the *Vastushastra*. These texts cover every aspect of architecture, from the selection of the site to the construction of the temple from the plinth to its spire. They give measurements and proportions for the different portions, images, and sculptural motifs that adorn the walls, pillars, and other areas.

Adornment (*alankara*) is an important feature of Indian culture. Decoration is considered to be auspicious, and the temple is adorned with various sculptural motifs such as creepers, birds, apsaras, *mithunas* (couples), and vyalas. These are considered to be magico-protective motifs, and are supposed to bring good luck.

The Puranas, those encyclopaedic works comprising Hindu myths and legends, also include architectural and iconic canons. One of the more important Puranas, the *Agni Purana* (c. ninth century AD), conceives of the temple as Purusha, the humanized Supreme Being. The terminology of the human body is applied to the temple. Thus, the base of the temple is its foot (*pada*), the wall is its thigh (*jangha*), and the spire its head (*mastaka* or shikhara). This terminology is still employed by present-day architectural historians in describing different parts of a temple.

The Khajuraho architects followed a particular Vastushastra tradition—that of the Vishvakarma school. This can be said on the basis of inscriptional evidence, although no actual text or manuscript has been discovered from this region. In the stone inscriptions of the temples, one often comes upon names of master-architects who followed the Vishvakarma tradition. Contrary to

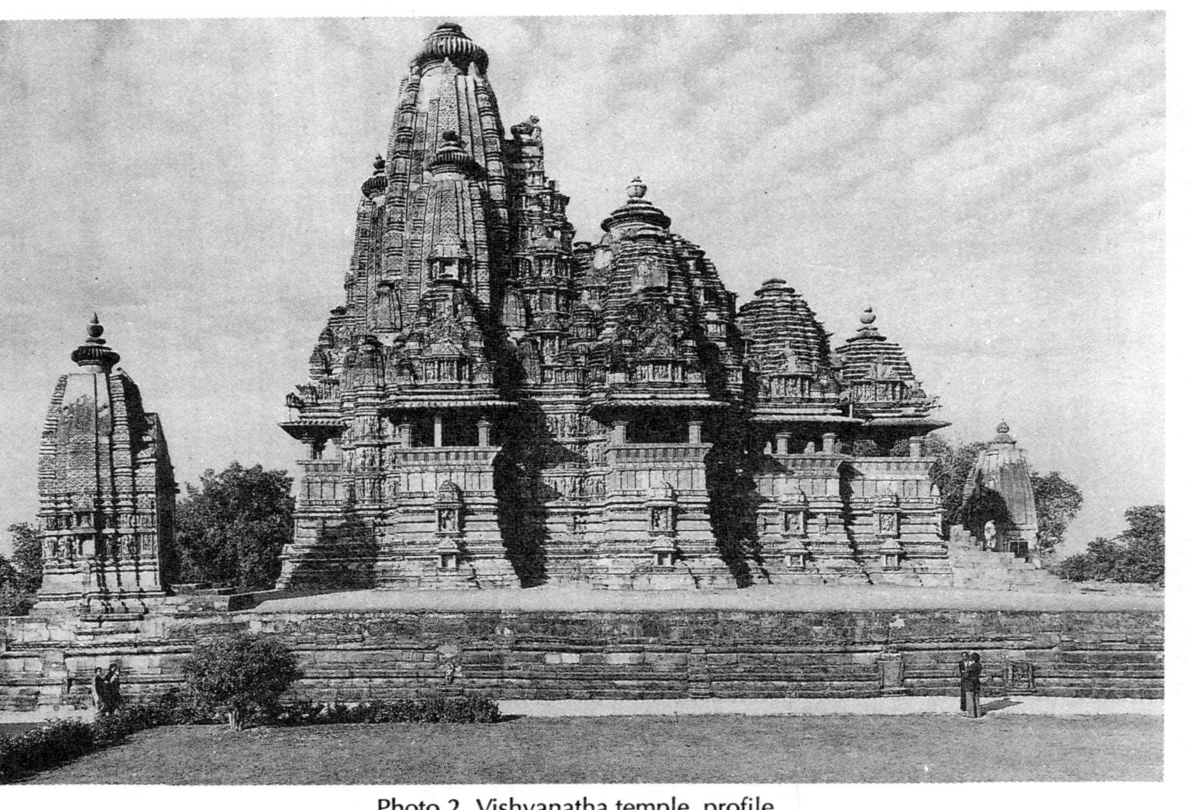

Photo 2. Vishvanatha temple, profile

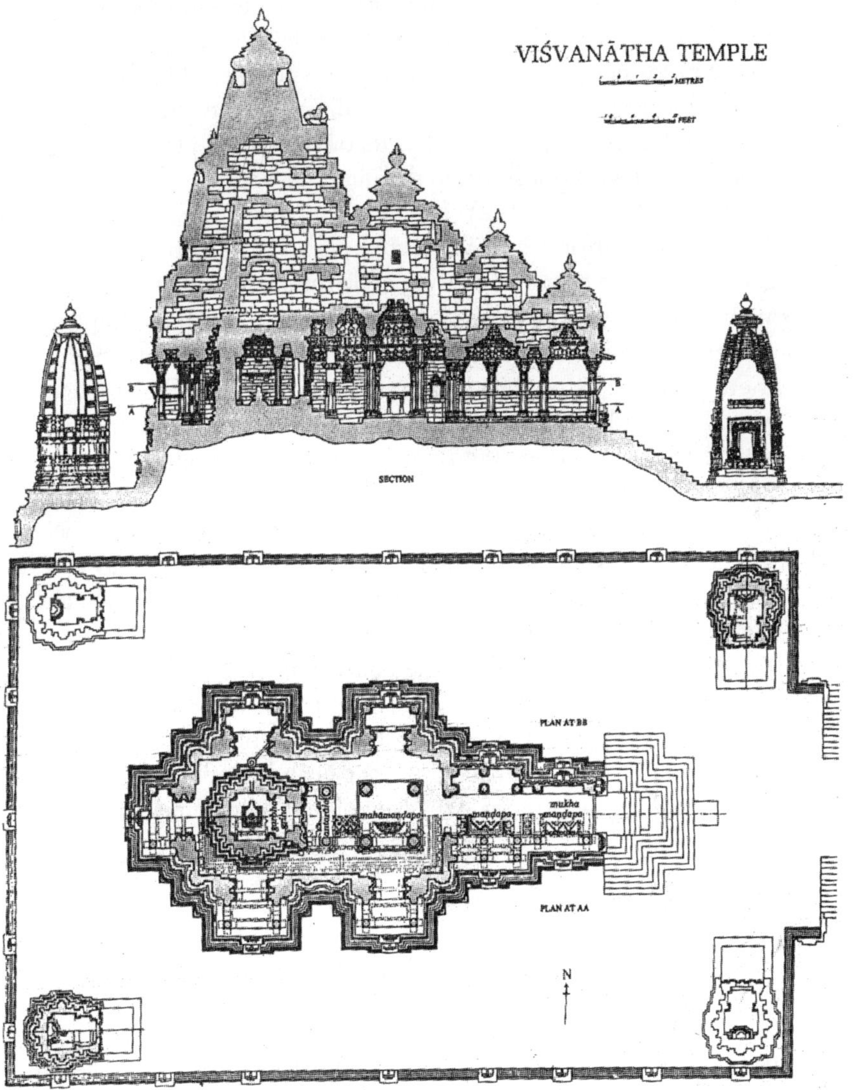

Fig. II. Plan and section of the Vishvanatha temple

general practice, the sculptors have left their signatures on more than a hundred sculptures and architraves, particularly in the Lakshmana and the Vishvanatha temples.

A highly evolved stage of Indian temple architecture is seen at Khajuraho. At least two of the larger temples—the Lakshmana and the Vishvanatha—are five-shrined (*panchayatana*), preserving subsidiary shrines in the four corners of the platform [**Fig. II**]. The Khajuraho temple has no enclosure walls, as in the case of south Indian and Orissan temples. It has its own separate platform that demarcates its sacred space from the material world.

The visitor approaches the temple after climbing several steps of the high platform and is greeted by an ornamented *torana* (gateway) at the entrance of the porch (mukhamandapa). Then, one walks into the hall (mandapa) and, in case of larger temples, to a big columnar hall (mahamandapa) with a square platform where sacred dances were performed in the past. The passage joining the hall and the sanctum is called antarala (vestibule). It is here that the devotee stands for *darshana* (visual perception) of the divinity enshrined in the sanctum.

The three larger Hindu temples—the Lakshmana, Vishvanatha, Kandariya Mahadeva—and the Jain Parshvanatha temple have an enclosed ambulatory (*pradakshina-patha*) around the sanctum. Such temples with a built-in inner ambulatory, are called *sandhara* temples [**Fig. III**]. Those without the built-in arrangement are called *nirandhara* temples [**Fig. IV**]. The devotee has to walk clockwise through this corridor around the sanctum, keeping it on his right side. Similarly, he circumambulates the entire temple, walking on its platform on the exterior. This symbolizes the circumambulation of the cosmos.

Elevation

The Khajuraho temple has three main divisions on its elevation: the plinth or basal story (pitha), the wall (jangha), and the roof or spire (shikhara). In addition to the tall platform (jagati) on which it stands, the temple has a high basal storey with a series of ornamental mouldings depicting human activities (narathara), masks of glory (grasapattika), and geometrical designs.

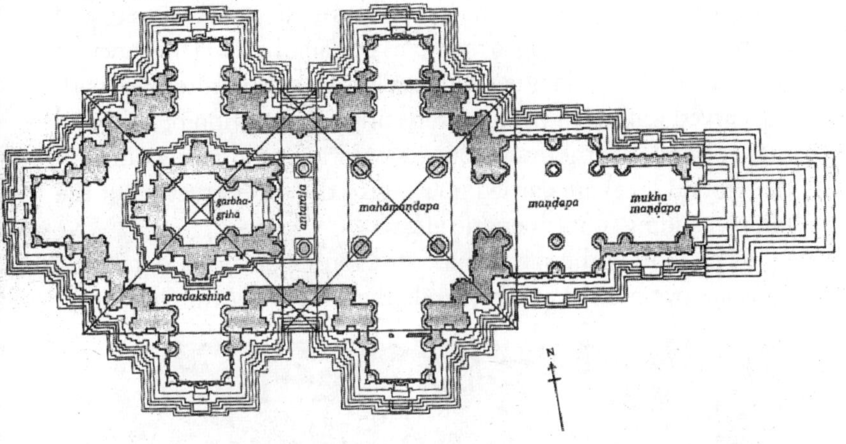

Fig. III. Plan of the Kandariya Mahadeva temple with inner ambulatory (*sandhara*)

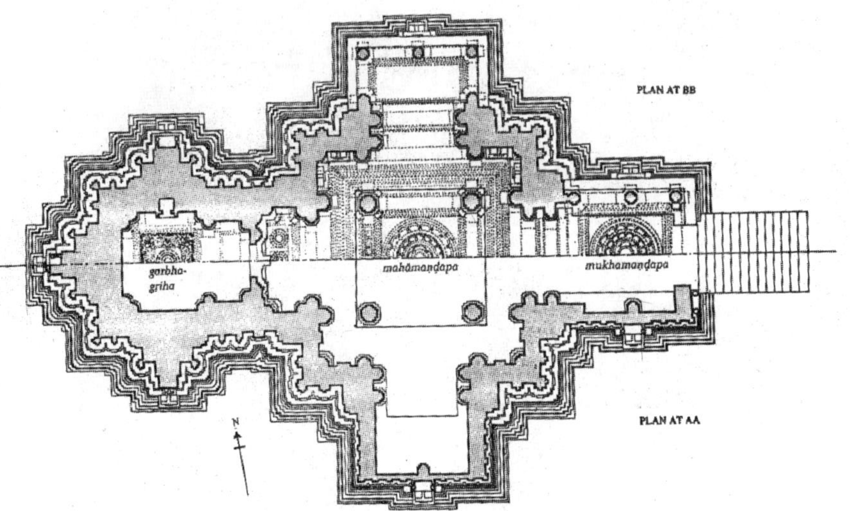

Fig. IV. Plan of the Devi Jagadamba temple without inner ambulatory (*nirandhara*)

Above the plinth is the wall section, jangha, divided into two or three sculptural zones [**Ph. 3**]. It is here that we see lovely figural sculptures—apsaras, griffins, couples or mithunas, guardian deities of space (*Dikpalas*), and so on. The famous erotic groups are situated on the portion of the jangha that joins the large hall and the sanctum [see **Ph. 9**]. The balconied windows of the temple alternate with the carved walls creating an interesting juxtaposition of light and shade. Similarly, the numerous indentations and projections on the ground level are carried upwards to the superstructure of the temple, adding to its dramatic effect.

The roofs of the subordinate structures such as the porch and halls are pyramidal in shape, while the tower over the sanctum is

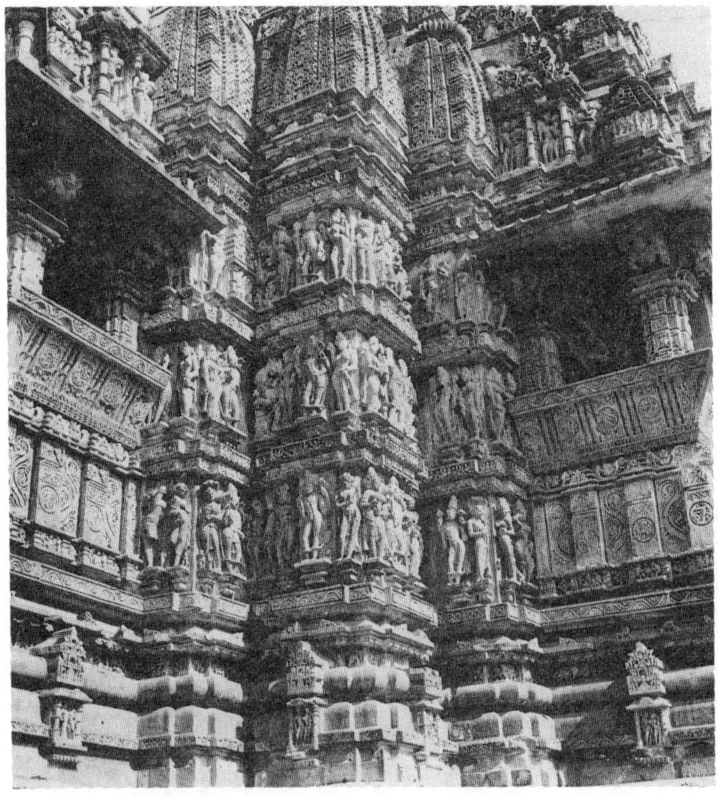

Photo 3. Harmony of sculpture and architecture, Vishvanatha temple

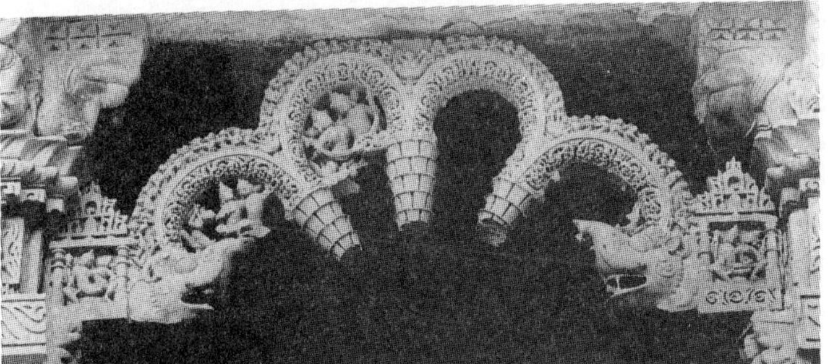

Photo 4. Arched gateway (torana), Kandariya Mahadeva temple

curvilinear, with graded peaks clustering around it. The architect has clearly emphasized the progressive ascent and descent of superstructures converging to the highest pinnacle, and has created a semblance of a mountain. In fact, inscriptions at Khajuraho compare the temple with Mount Kailasa, the abode of Shiva, or Mount Meru, the centre of the Universe. The architectural imagery of the Khajuraho temples indeed helps us to conceive of the temple as the centre of the universe.

Interiors

The temple at Khajuraho is also lavishly carved in its interior. The Lakshmana, Kandariya, and Javari temples still preserve arched gateways or toranas decorated with makaras, mythic aquatic animals [**Ph. 4**]. The ceilings of the halls and vestibule are carved with intricate geometric and floral designs. The pillar brackets bear high-reliefed sculptures of vyalas alternating with woman-and-tree (*shalabhanjika*) figures and surasundaris in various activities such as playing with a ball, displaying love marks, wearing ornaments, and holding a mirror. The sanctum doorway is decorated with conventional auspicious motifs: mithunas, creepers, dwarfs. It is guarded by door-keepers (dvarapalas), and 'purified' by the river goddesses, Ganga and Yamuna sculpted in human form.

In the large temples (Lakshmana, Vishvanatha, Kandariya), the plan of the cella, with its inner ambulatory, resembles a three-dimensional yantra, with the eight corners guarded by the Dikpalas and Vasus. The three cardinal niches represent the manifestations of the main divinity enshrined in the sanctum. The recesses bear the figures of sinuous vyalas, while the projections display surasundaris and couples. On the sanctum wall of the Lakshmana temple [**Fig. V**], there are eight Dikpalas and eight Vasus in the corners, twelve panels depicting Krishna-lila and twelve vyalas in the recesses, twenty-four surasundaris on the projections, and the incarnations of Vishnu in the three cardinal niches.

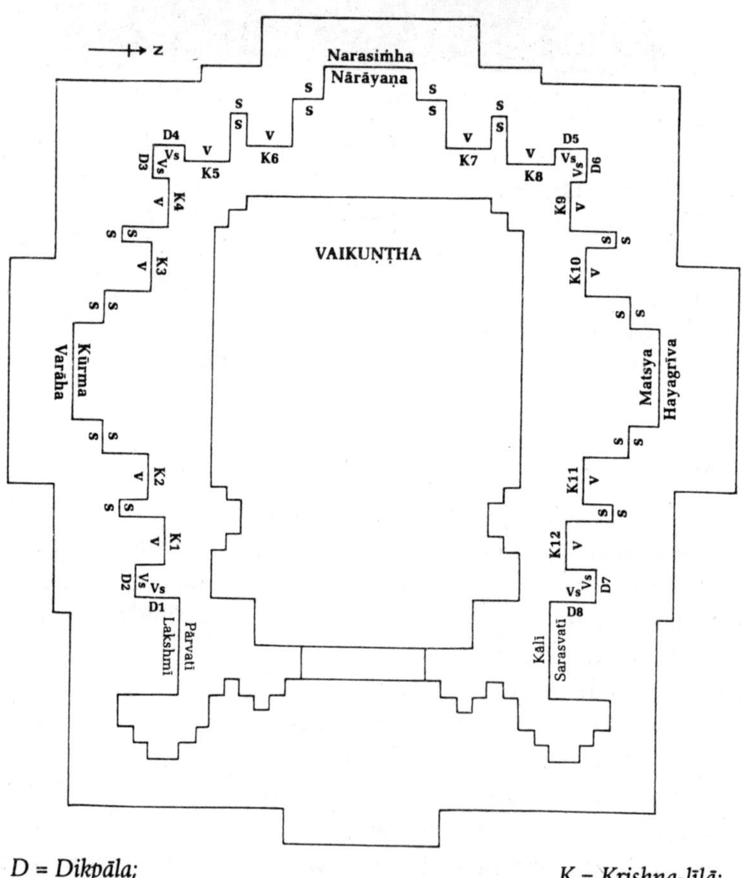

D = Dikpāla;
D1 = Indra; D2 = Agni; D3 = Yama; D4 = Nirṛiti;
D5 = Varuṇa; D6 = Vāyu; D7 = Kubera; D8 = Īśāna.

K = Kṛishṇa-līlā;
S = surasundarī.
V = vyāla.
Vs = Vasu.

Fig. V. Placement of images on the sanctum wall, Lakshmana temple

FIVE

Sculpture:
Themes and Meanings

Distinctive Features

The sculptures in the Khajuraho temples are made of finely grained stone ranging from pale buff to pink, yellow, and brown. The stone has a softness that lends to smoothness in carving. The human body is shown in its sensuous charm in a variety of postures and attitudes. The figures are not muscular as in classical Greek sculpture; the beauty of the human form is revealed from many angles through diaphanous clothes.

The 'classical' Indian quality and subtle warmth of modelling is reflected in the sculptures of the early temples, such as the Lakshmana [**Ph. 5**] and the Parshvanatha, of the mid-tenth century. The artist of the Vishvanatha temple presents perfectly proportioned and poised figures [see **Ph. 8**]. The temples which follow in time—the Devi Jagadamba and the Chitragupta—retain the rounded modelling and the graceful forms. In the Kandariya Mahadeva, the figures become slender and tall, and some of them revolve round their own axis. The mass production of sculptures

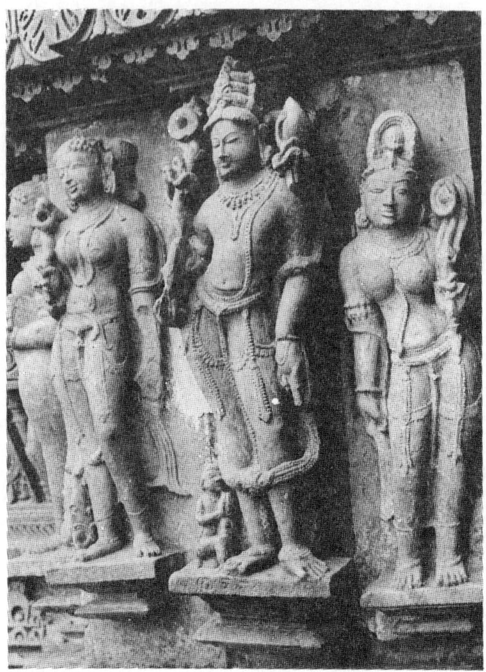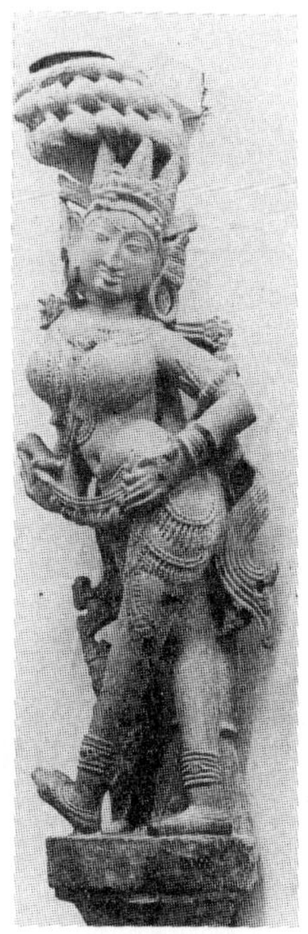

Photo 5. Vishnu, and celestial women, on the exterior wall, the Lakshmana temple

Photo 6. Female figure from Duladeva temple, ASI Museum

in this architecturally magnificent monument affects the quality of the figures. The 'medieval' concept of form influences the last of the Khajuraho series—the Duladeva temple. In this temple, built in c. AD 1130, we find a sharp angularity of limbs and bodies, pointed facial features and lavish ornamention [**Ph. 6**]. The icons of this temple have lost their vitality, yet some of the flying figures on the wall and the bracket statues are quite lively.

The sculptures at Khajuraho are harmoniously integrated with architecture and add to the rhythm of the monuments. Whether one is acquainted with its iconographic significance or not, it is hard not to be impressed by the unified design of the temple, with its horizontal bands of sculpture perfectly balanced with the rising verticality of the building. Moreover, a rhythmic pattern is conveyed in the arrangement of the sculptures on the temple walls. Each temple has its own pattern of arranging sculptural motifs: in the Lakshmana temple, surasundaris on the projections alternate with vyalas in recesses of the walls [see **Fig. V**]. The hundreds of divinities carved on the walls and niches of the inner halls are conceptually integrated with the central divinity enshrined in the sanctum. Each sculpture is part of the whole; a part of a preconceived order.

Main Categories

Subject-wise, the sculptures in the Khajuraho temples can be classified into eight categories:

1) **The cult icons** installed in the sanctum. These are generally executed in the round, and in accordance with prescribed conventions of *Shilpa* texts. They have a nimbus and a paraphernalia of attending figures, hierarchically arranged in frames of steles. The best specimen is undoubtedly the 2.75 m. (9 ft.) high image in the Chaturbhuja temple [see **Ph. 24**], expressing communion with his devotees through his gentle smile. This exceptional cult icon is executed in *tribhanga* (three bends of the body), while the icons in other temples stand erect in *samabhanga*. The colossal statue of Parvati performing penance, now in the Museum, and those of the Jain Tirthankaras in meditative postures are also noteworthy.

2) **The attendant and surrounding divinities** executed in round or high relief. Those seen in the cardinal niches [see **Ph. 18**] of the temples are generally vital figures, believed to radiate the power of the central divinity of the sanctum. The images of the Dikpalas, in the eight directions of the temple, and those of Shiva and Vishnu [see **Ph. 5**] on the exterior walls stand with ease in tribhanga. They carry weapons in their hands in accordance with the canonical texts. They look like humans, but are distinguished by the *shrivatsa* (diamond-like mark) on their chests, crowned head-dresses, long garlands reaching below the knees, and their *vahanas* (mounts) at their feet.

3) **The demi-gods** such as the vidyadharas, gandharvas, ganas. These are dynamic figures generally carved on the top row of the wall, symbolizing the celestial world. The flying vidyadharas hold

garlands and flank the divinities. The playful ganas are found on door jambs and pedestals of Shaivite images. As load-bearing, four-armed dwarfs, they are seen on the pillar brackets of all the temples, some of them with funny expressions on their faces.

4) **Celestial women** called apsaras or surasundaris, engaged in various activities, presented by the Chandella artists in front, back and side views, carved in the round or in high relief.

5) **Amorous couples** or mithunas, and erotic groups, related to the auspicious symbolism of early Indian art, acquire added importance at Khajuraho.

6) **Secular scenes** in reliefs depicting the royal hunt, the king at court, marching armies, domestic scenes, teacher and pupils, dance processions, a dancer conversing with an Acharya [**Ph. 7**], sculptors at work, traders with camels, and others. These themes are shown in relief panels placed on the jagati (platform) of the Lakshmana temple and on the narathara row on the plinth of the temples.

7) **Animal figures,** both mythical and realistic, which include the

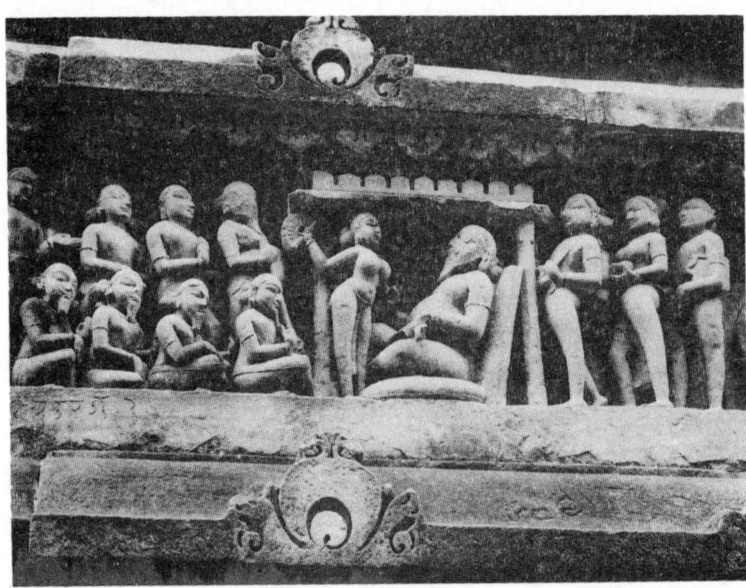

Photo 7. Dancer conversing with an Acharya, platform, Lakshmana temple

vyala [**Phs. 8, 23**], a fabulous creature with a lion's body and the head of different creatures such as a parrot, an elephant, a boar and others. The vyala is a typical motif of medieval temple art and is very popular at Khajuraho. Elephants are depicted in a row on the basement of the Lakshmana temple and as large figures in the round, placed near the entrance of the Vishvanatha temple. One of the most magnificent animal representations is Nandi, Shiva's bull, carved from a single huge stone, and sheltered in a specially built mandapa (pavilion), facing the Vishvanatha temple.

8) **Geometric and floral designs** are carved on the ceilings, on the borders of panels and walls, on pillars and elsewhere. The lotus is an important motif in ceiling decorations and on pedestals of divinities.

Some of the sculptural themes at Khajuraho are described below:

Celestial Women (apsaras, surasundaris)

The medieval temples of India, including those at Khajuraho, have a preponderance of female figures in their sculptural scheme. They are represented on walls, pillar-brackets and other architectural parts of the temple. The women indulge in various everyday activities such as applying make-up, removing a thorn from the foot, tying or untying the waist girdle, rinsing water from wet hair, writing a letter, playing a game of ball, carrying a baby, and dancing [**Phs. 6, 8, 21**]. The medieval *Vastu* texts specifically ordain the carving of female figures on temple walls. The Orissan text *Shilpa Prakasha* (I, 392) states:

As a house without a wife, as frolic without a woman, so without a figure of a woman the monument will be of inferior quality and bear no fruit.

This text describes 16 types of female figures in various activities such as *nupurapadika*, one with ankle bells, *darpana*, one with a mirror, and so on. The classification becomes more elaborate in the fifteenth century, when we get detailed descriptions of thirty-two types of female figures in the western Indian text *Kshirarnava*.

The temples contemporaneous with Khajuraho, such as those

at Jagat, Suhania, Modhera, and Bhubaneswar also depict a variety of female figures. They are, in fact, ubiquitous. The apsaras and surasundaris of Khajuraho and other medieval temples are auspicious motifs whose origin can be traced to vegetation spirits (*Yakshis*) and fertility figures of early Indian art at Sanchi, Bharhut and Mathura.

One of the favourite motifs of the Khajuraho artists is the surasundari undressing to remove a scorpion from her body [**Ph. 8**]. This was a poetic device used to express fertility. Female nudity was regarded as a potent fertility charm. On another level, one of the Sanskrit words for scorpion is '*kharjura*', and this could be related to the ancient name of Khajuraho, i.e. Kharjura-vahaka, which means: 1) date-palm-bearing, 2) scorpion-bearing. The scorpion-bearing female figure is, as it were, the emblem of the town Kharjura-vahaka.

Erotic Figures

Khajuraho is famous for its erotic sculptures. But one must remember that erotic figures do not even account for one-tenth of the site's sculptures, most of which represent divinities, celestial females, and mythic animals. Moreover, erotic figures are depicted on most temples of India built between AD 900 and 1300, and are represented according to the sculptural scheme of the region in which they are situated.

At Khajuraho, erotic figures are placed on the main wall portion (jangha) of the temples and therefore are large—about a metre in height—and graceful [**Ph. 21**], thus drawing immediate attention to themselves. In the temples of western and southern India (Gujarat, Maharashtra, and Karnataka), on the other hand, they are located on smaller rows of the plinth, below eye level, or on balcony panels (*kakshasana*), and hence, although they portray more sensual themes, they do not attract the notice of visitors as do the larger figures on the temple walls of Khajuraho, Puri, Bhubanesvar, and Konarak.

One must not forget that the convention of depicting erotic figures was not invented by the artists of Khajuraho. It was part of

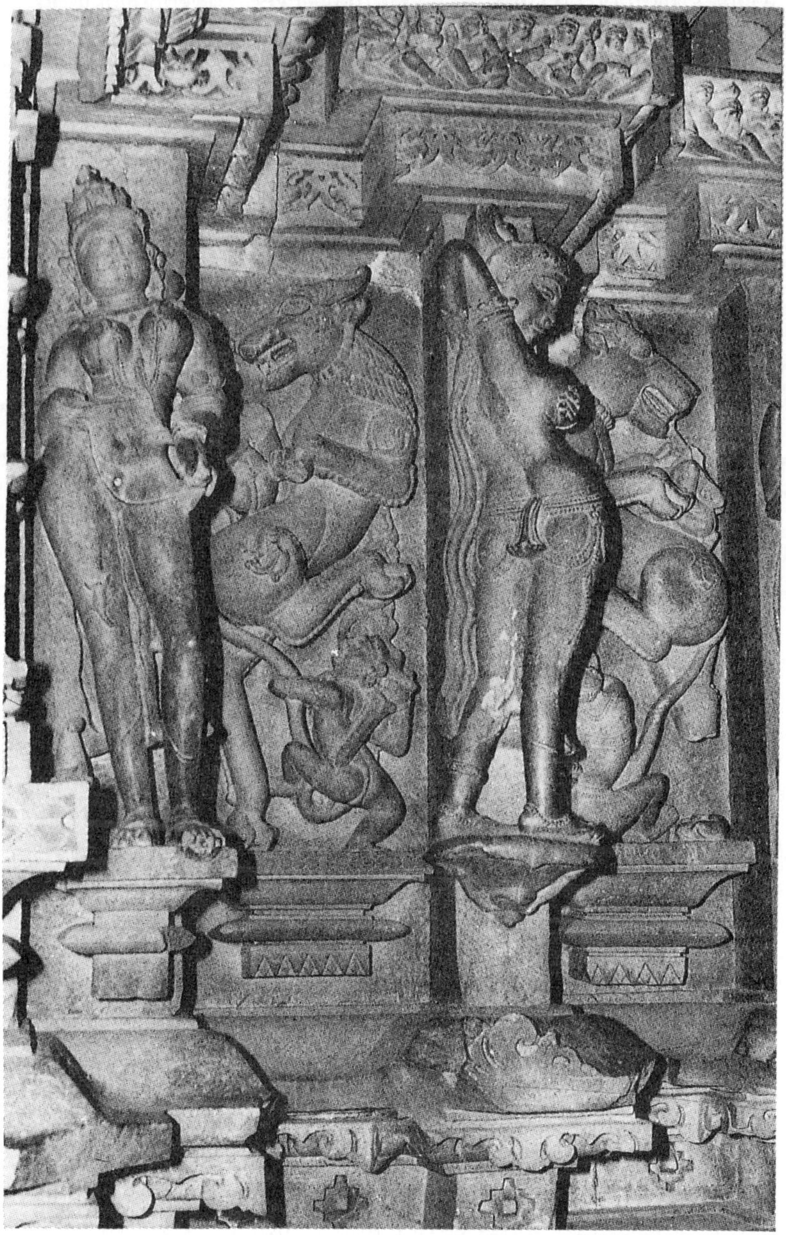

Photo 8. *Apsaras* and *vyalas*, sanctum wall, Vishvanatha temple

a larger tradition prevalent at an all-India level. The configuration of various factors that led to erotic depiction in Indian art from the first century BC to the thirteenth century AD has been discussed at length by me in my monograph, *The Erotic Sculpture of India— A Socio-Cultural Study*.

There are several hypotheses that attempt to explain the presence of sensual figures in religious art. The argument that erotic figures represent *kama* (desire), the third *purushartha* (aim of life), or that they were designed to test the spiritual strength of the Yogis, or that they were intended for sex education, does not stand in the face of the variety and types of figures displayed in the temples.

Erotic motifs occur in the art of all three religious sects— Hindu, Buddhist and Jain—and arise out a common substratum of magico-religious beliefs and practices associated with fertility cults. Rites of fertility involved actual sexual practice or its symbolic representation. The word 'fertility' is employed here to include not only its primary purpose of procreation but also its wider connotations: the aversion of evil, death and misfortune, and the promotion of life, happiness, prosperity, and auspiciousness.

The *Shilpashastras* and other authoritative texts on temple art have recognized both the auspicious and protective aspects of erotic figures. The *Brihat Samhita* of the sixth century AD clearly ordains that mithunas (couples) should 'decorate' the temple door, along with creepers, ganas (goblins), and other auspicious and luck-bringing motifs. Erotic motifs were considered alankara, protective and auspicious (*shubha, mangala*) in function

Gradually, with changing socio-religious conditions and the increasing influence of Tantric practices, the fertility aspects of erotic sculptures were reinforced. Between AD 600 and 900, coital couples were depicted in temple art but this theme was not too frequent. From AD 900 onwards, the ruling dynasties of the feudal age competed with one another in displaying their wealth and power by building larger and more lavishly decorated temples. It was at this time that the portrayal of erotic figures proliferated. Many temples in India built between AD 900–1300 blatantly display erotic themes. Khajuraho is one such site, among many others, one may add.

People often interpret the Khajuraho sculptures as depicting the art of love-making as described in the *Kamasutra* of Vatsyayana. In a recent international documentary, Khajuraho is erroneously called 'the temple of *Kamasutra*'. Vatsyayana, who composed this manual, lived in the fourth century AD, 600 years before the period of the Khajuraho temples. Although the *Kamasutra* and other manuals of love were studied by the cultural elite of India, the depiction of erotic figures on religious buildings does not seem to have originated in a secular interest in sex manuals. Erotic figures on the temples of Khajuraho, Bhubanesvar, and other sites belong to a totally different tradition, where both religious and worldy interests could merge. They have to be distinguished from those depicted in the illustrated manuscripts of the later period. Khajuraho's sculptures were not primarily created to illustrate the various postures described in sex manuals. The themes depicted in the temples could not, by any stretch of imagination, be for sex education. It could be possible that the sculptors, like their counterparts the literary artists and poets, displayed their knowledge of the *Kamasutra* or a similar manual. It is interesting to note that the temple artists have depicted couples performing oral sex, a posture that is condemned in the *Kamasutra*. Just like the Sanskrit poets of the period, the sculptors have also made fun of ascetics of rival sects by portraying them in this condemnatory posture.

The view that the Khajuraho temples belonged to apparently hedonistic religious sects like the Kapalikas, who expressed their philosophy through erotic art, is also not tenable. There is no evidence to support the association of the Kapalikas with temple management. The sculptures do represent scenes which show ascetics and royal personages participating in orgies. These scenes may indicate possible situations known or imagined by the artists, but the temple builders were not likely to display themselves in lurid sexual practices. It is possible, therefore, that the royal and ascetic figures are deliberately used to mock certain debased practices of extreme Tantric sects. This attitude is reflected in the Sanskrit literature of the period as well.

Erotic figures first appear at Khajuraho in AD 950, on its earliest temple built in the elite Nagara style of architecture—the Lakshmana, dedicated to Vishnu-Vaikuntha. By this time, Indian architects were quite familiar with the use of erotic motifs in temple art as an auspicious ornament (alankara), protective in function. At Khajuraho, the architects assign erotic motifs to the following places: the door-jamb of the sanctum; the narathara or human activities row of the plinth; the row of the jagati or platform along with royal pastimes, battle scenes, and dancers; the recesses of the jangha; and niches of the superstructure. Couples are also placed round the images of Matrikas (Mothers) in the two Shiva temples— the Vishvanatha and the Kandariya Mahadeva—which brings to mind a similar practice followed in the temples of Gujarat and Rajasthan. The Mothers were said to be appeased by the performance of the procreative act, or its substitution. The depiction of erotic figures is a substitute for the actual act.

What, however, draws the attention of a keen observer at Khajuraho is not the variety of erotic subjects centering around ascetics and aristocrats and their frequent and loud display, but also their peculiar placement in the sculptural scheme of the temples. The architect has placed erotic sculptures on the wall portion between the two balconies in the three major Hindu sandhara temples [**Ph. 9**]. This wall portion is actually the architectural juncture of the big hall (mahamandapa), and the sanctum (garbhagriha) [see **Fig. III**]. Here, the architect has employed puns and intentional language, called *sandhya bhasha*. This is a code language used by esoteric religious practitioners and Tantric texts to conceal their doctrines from outsiders. This enigmatic language employs erotic terminology to convey non-communicable experiences, which cannot be expressed in ordinary language. For instance, when one reads: 'A washerwoman clings to the Yogi (ascetic) on his neck', it is found to be erotic if taken literally. But in the code language of the Tantras, it means that the washerwoman, i.e. Dombi=Kundalini energy, has ascended to the *chakra* (subtle centre) of the neck. Similarly, erotic figures on temple walls could be metaphoric and might conceal a deeper symbolism.

There are two notable head-down postures on the juncture walls of the two Shiva temples in the Western group. Their

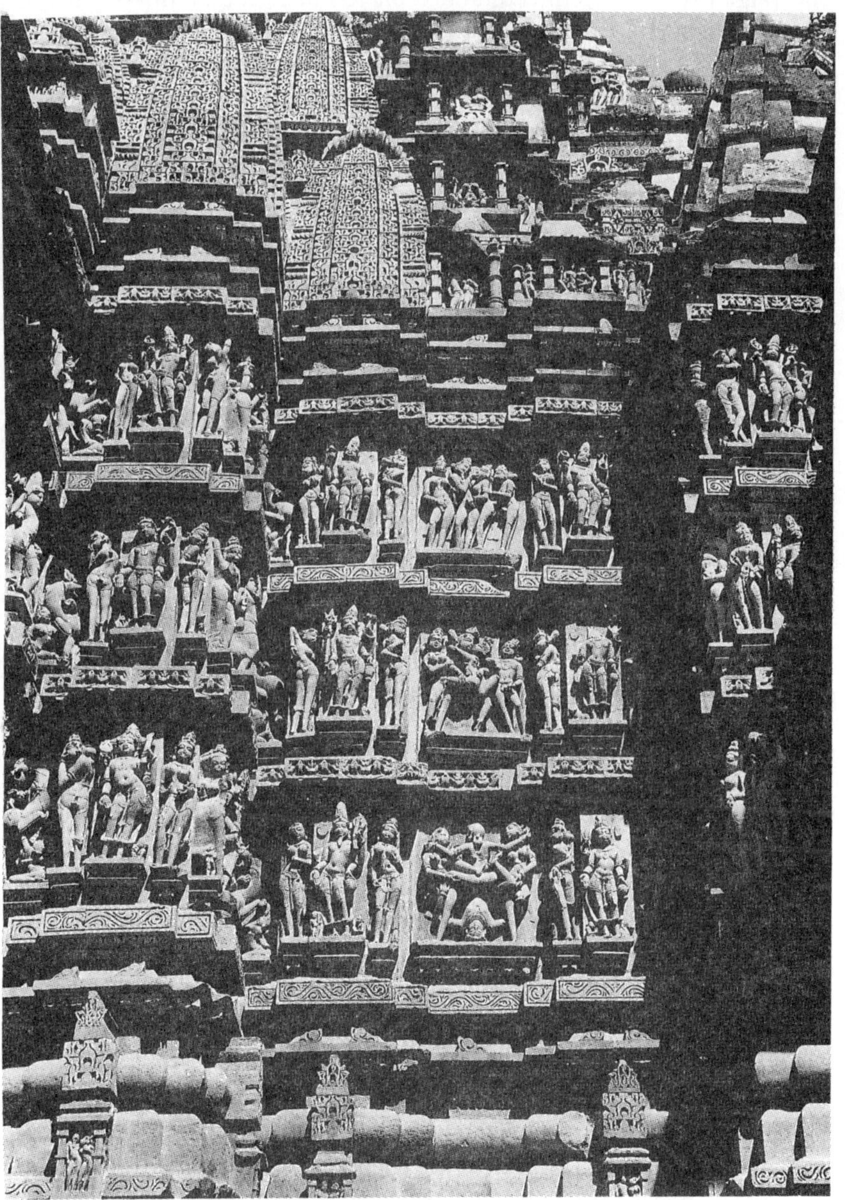

Photo 9. Sculptures on the juncture wall, Kandariya Mahadeva

composition [**Ph.10**] is remarkably similar to the *Kamakala Yantra* [**Fig. VI**] of the architectural text *Shilpa Prakasha* (c. tenth–twelfth century AD). This text states that such a yantra is to be placed on temples for magico-propitiatory purposes. It would defend the temple against calamities and evil spirits. But the lines of the yantra have to be hidden from the gaze of non-initiated persons by covering them with erotic figures, which in turn would 'delight' lay persons.

Thus, the erotic figures of Khajuraho have multiple functions: 1) They are magico-defensive and auspicious motifs, as elsewhere in Indian art. 2) They 'delight' lay visitors. 3) They possibly conceal a yantra beneath the head-down posture images on the juncture walls of the two Shiva temples. 4) They seem to embody some yogic-philosophic meaning or concept through sandhya bhasha in the juncture wall panels of the three major temples of the Western group. In terms of Yoga, they could symbolically represent the process of the unification of the two breaths, *prana* and *apana*, inhalation and exhalation, the combining of two polar opposites, which leads to the non-conditioned timeless state of non-duality. (For more details, see Mircea Eliade, *Yoga: Immortality and Freedom*, Chapter VI; Devangana Desai, *The Religious Imagery of Khajuraho*, Chapter VII, 'Puns and Enigmatic Language in Sculpture.')

Attitude toward Sexuality and Women: It may be appropriate here to discuss the sexual mores of the period. At the social level there was a double standard for the genders. Men could enjoy sex with as many women as they could afford, financially and physically, and according to their status, whereas the married women of high society were confined to their polygamous husbands. There was no 'free love' in the period, as some may naively imagine to be the case from the explicit display of sex in the art of the temples. High society ladies generally stayed indoors in their own apartments, not accessible to outsiders. Some of the Chandella queens, however, seem to have taken interest in charitable work. The Chief Queen enjoyed a distinctive position in the royal court. Chandella inscriptions cite examples of ideal women from Puranic tales, such as Arundhati and Anasuya, and their devotion to their husbands. Social codes were strict on extramarital affairs, though literature and the arts paint a more romantic picture. Low caste women,

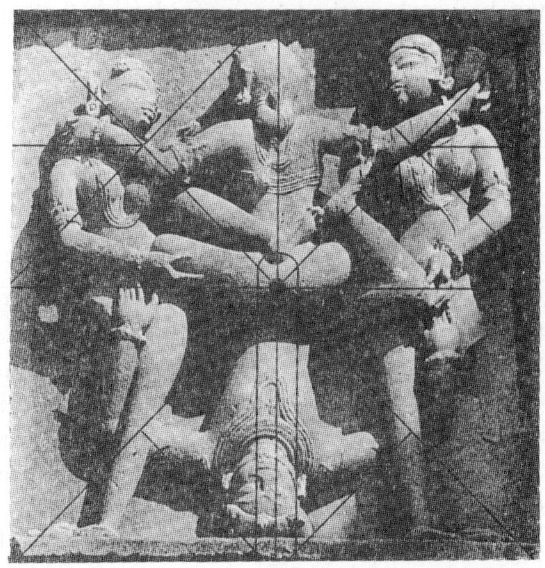

Photo 10. Head-down posture, with lines of the *Kamakala-Yantra* superimposed

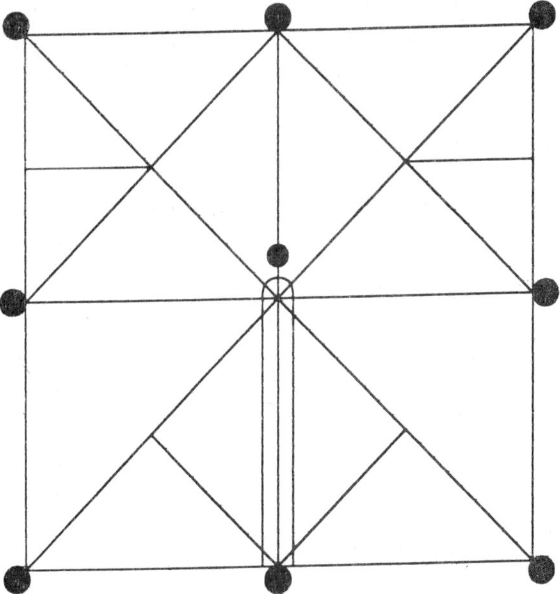

Fig. VI. Lines of the *Kamakala-Yantra* (After *Shilpa Prakasha*)

however, had comparatively more freedom in their sex lives, but exploitation cannot be ruled out.

On the whole, women were respected and those belonging to the upper classes owned personal property. They were able to make donations for the construction of temples, wells, and other public buildings, and give charities to Brahmins. There is mention of queen Satyabhama who made donations to Brahmins on the day of a solar eclipse. Another Chandella queen, Kalyanadevi, built a well and a rest-house for pilgrims. She was educated and she arranged to get the genealogy of her husband's and that of her father's family inscribed. The chief dancer, Padmavati, at the Chandella fort Kalanjar is also known to have made donations to the Shiva temple. The *varastris*, 'the best among women', as an inscription mentions, presented gifts to the Kandariya Mahadeva temple on some special occasion.

The beauty of young maidens was appreciated and admired in public assemblies as suggested in the literature of the period and in the sensuous carvings of apsaras and surasundaris on temple walls. The play *Karpuramanjari*, written by the poet Rajashekhara, of the neighbouring Pratihara court, in the tenth century, brings on stage a bathing heroine to reveal her charms.

Mythical Creatures

Vyala: Originally derived from Persian art, this composite creature, with the body of a lion and the face of an elephant, goat, parrot or other animals and birds, was known in India from at least the second century BC. It enjoyed a great popularity in medieval Indian temples. The vyala was considered to be a protective motif, and placed in recesses of the wall [see **Ph.8**], and on the brackets of pillars, at Khajuraho. A warrior is often depicted fighting a rampant vyala. Medieval texts describe several varieties of vyala figures. The twelfth century Vastu text *Aparajitaprichcha* mentions sixteen varieties of vyalas with faces of different creatures, and adds that there are further variations due to their diverse body forms. The Parshvanatha [see **Ph.23**] and the Devi Jagadamba temples have a number of different vyala figures on their outer walls.

Makara: This mythical aquatic creature combines the jaws of a crocodile, trunk of an elephant, ears of a lion, horns of a ram, and the tail of fish. It is the mount of the river goddess Ganga, and also of the Dikpala Varuna. One can find makaras on the torana-gates of the Kandariya [see **Ph. 4**] and other temples, on arched frames of divinities, on water chutes (*pranala*), and in many other places in Khajuraho.

Icons: Hindu Divinities

The Khajuraho temples were dedicated to Vishnu, Shiva, Surya, and the Yoginis. Here are some brief descriptions of those deities, as well as of Ganesha, Karttikeya, Parvati, the Grahas (Planets), and the Seven Matrikas, whose images one will find in the niches of the temples. The Khajuraho artists have created some extraordinary images of these divinities, which express deep philosophical concepts.

Vishnu: The god who preserves the universe, Vishnu is associated with royalty and regal power. He assumes periodic *avataras* (incarnations) in order to overthrow evil. Although all his ten standard avataras are represented at Khajuraho, only Vishnu himself, and three of his avataras, are enshrined in the temples. These are Varaha, the Boar [see **Ph.14**], who lifts the Earth Goddess out of the nether region; Vamana, the Dwarf; and Vaikuntha, a composite form, with faces of a Boar (Varaha) and a lion (Narasimha), along with a human face [see **Ph. 17**]. There is also a four-faced Vaikuntha, with an additional face of a horse, now in the ASI Museum.

The other avataras represented in niches or panels are: Matsya (Fish), Kurma (Tortoise), Narasimha (Man-Lion), Parashurama, Rama, Balarama, Krishna, Buddha, and Kalki (the Future incarnation). Hayagriva, the horse-necked avatara associated with learning, who saves the Vedas from the demons, is placed in cardinal niches of the Lakshmana and the Vamana temples.

Among the great images at Khajuraho are those of Vishnu as Yogeshvara, seated in the *padmasana* posture, giving discourse to sages, placed in the upper cardinal niches of the Lakshmana temple [see **Ph.18**]. Vishnu making a gesture of silence with his forefinger near his lips is one unique sculpture (now in the ASI Museum), not found anywhere else in Asia.

Shiva: In case of the Shiva temples, it is always the linga, his emblem, considered to be the sign of the unmanifest Supreme Shiva, that is installed in the exact centre of the sanctum. Shiva's manifestations are placed in the three cardinal niches of the sanctum, in the hall, and on the exterior walls of the temple.

Both placid and terrific manifestations of Shiva are represented at Khajuraho. These are: Natesha (Cosmic Dancer), Kalyana-Sundara (Bridegroom), Ardhanarishvara (Androgyn), Uma-Maheshvara (seated with Uma), Uma-Alingana Murti (embracing Uma in a standing posture), Andhakasuravadha Murti (slaying the Blind Demon), Tripurantaka (vanquishing the three cities of demons), Bhairava, the fierce aspect, and others.

Of these, the most important is Sadashiva, the manifest-unmanifest (*sakala-nishkala*) aspect of Shiva, who is the pivot of the iconic scheme of the Kandariya Mahadeva temple. Two unique sculptures of Sadashiva at Khajuraho [**Ph.11**] depict him

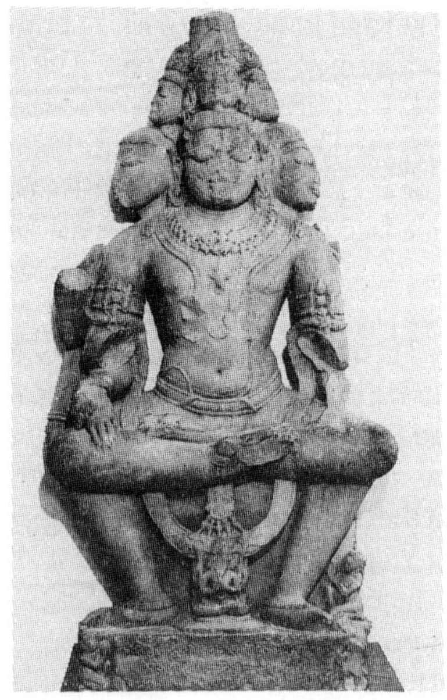

Photo 11. Sadashiva image, ASI Museum

with four feet (*chatushpadas*). There is a pun on the word pada, which means foot, but can also mean quarter part of a text. The four-footed image of Sadashiva metaphorically suggests the four parts (padas) of the texts of the Shaiva Siddhanta sect, associated with Khajuraho.

Brahma: Considered to be the creator god among the triad (Brahma, Vishnu, Shiva), Brahma, however, has no temple dedicated to him at Khajuraho. The so-called 'Brahma' temple originally was a Vishnu temple. But Brahma is shown as a subsidiary figure in both Vishnu and Shiva temples. Portrayed as four-headed (of which three heads are visible) and with a beard, he holds in his right hand a rosary while displaying the boon-giving gesture (*varada mudra*), while in his other hands he holds a ladle, a book and a pot (*kalasha*). His mount is the *hamsa* (goose).

Surya: The Sun god is shown in human form, generally standing in samabhanga, wearing shoes and dressed like a northerner. He holds a lotus in each of his hands, signifying the creation of life. Seven horses are depicted as pulling his chariot. At Khajuraho, there is a separate shrine dedicated to Surya, now called the Chitragupta temple.

Parvati / Uma: Goddess, daughter of Parvata (mountain) and wife of Shiva. Her independent images show her standing in equipoise—samabhanga—and performing *tapas* (penance), with an iguana (*godha*) as her mount. Her colossal image in the Museum indicates that it must have once been enshrined in a temple.

Yoginis: Considered to be manifestations or companions of the Great Goddess, the Yoginis, sixty four in number, were worshipped collectively in an open-air granite sanctuary at Khajuraho [see **Ph. 22**]. Today, however, their cells are bereft of images. The three images mentioned by Major Cunningham are now in the Museum.

Durga: The warrior goddess is shown as slaying Mahishasura, the buffalo demon. She is accompanied by her mount, a lion. The image in the principal cell of the Chausath Yogini temple at the time of Cunningham's visit was Mahishasuramardini (now in the open-air Museum of the ASI).

Lakshmi: The goddess of wealth and beauty, she is the consort of Vishnu. She is depicted as annointed by two elephants and holds a lotus in each of her two upper hands.

Sarasvati: The goddess of learning and wisdom, she is generally paired with Lakshmi at Khajuraho. She is depicted as holding a musical instrument, the *vina*, with two hands, while two other hands hold a lotus and a book.

Karttikeya: Son of Shiva and Parvati, he is a war god. At Khajuraho, however, he is also a teacher of grammar, and is shown holding a manuscript in one hand.

Ganesha: This popular god, easy to identify because of his elephant face and pot belly, has many images at Khajuraho, and is found in almost all the temples. He is generally represented in a dance posture [see **Ph. 25**], or shown seated or standing, with a rat as his mount. Ganesha is believed to remove obstacles and is propitiated at the beginning of some auspicious work or ritual.

The Seven Matrikas: The Mothers, represented collectively at Khajuraho, in their respective *krama* (order) are: Brahmani, Maheshvari, Kaumari [see **Ph. 20**], Vaishnavi, Varahi, Aindri, and Chamunda. They signify the powers of the gods created to assist Shiva and Devi in their battles against the demons. They are generally shown as dancing, seated, or standing on door lintels, jambs, and niches of temples. They are accompanied by Shiva in the form of Virabhadra, and Ganesha.

The Nava Grahas: The nine planets are shown standing or seated on the door lintels of the sanctums of temples of all sects, including the Jain.

Icons: The Jain Tirthankaras and Divinities

The Jain temples of Khajuraho are associated with the Digambara sect. By the tenth century, the Jain pantheon had become quite elaborate. At Khajuraho, there are images of 1) Jinas or Tirthankaras, 2) Yakshas and Yakshis, who are guardian deities (*shasana-devatas*) subservient to the Jinas, and who grant the mundane wishes of devotees, 3) Vidyadevis (goddesses of knowledge), 4) Kshetrapalas,

Photo 12. Jain
Tirthankara Adinatha,
ASI Museum

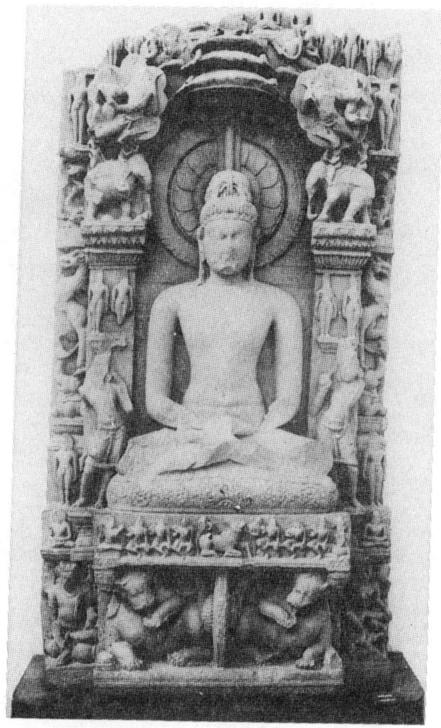

and 5) other deities such as Grahas and Dikpalas, as in the Hindu temples.

Jinas or Tirthankaras: Jina means victorious, the perfected being. The Jina or Tirthankara images are the nucleus of the Jain temples. There are as many as two hundred images of Jinas at Khajuraho. Of the twenty-four Jinas, at least fifteen are represented here. The largest number of images, about sixty, are those of Adinatha or Rishabhanatha [**Ph. 12**], the first Jina. Parshvanatha, the twenty-third Jina, is represented in twenty images; Mahavira, the twenty-fourth Jina, in nine, and Shantinatha, the sixteenth Jina, has four images, one of which is 4.3 meters (14 ft.) tall.

As elsewhere in India, the Jinas are portrayed only in the two passionless meditative postures: seated in padmasana (lotus-seat); and standing erect in *kayotsarga*, without any bend of the body. At Khajuraho they are shown seated on *simhasana* (lion's seat),

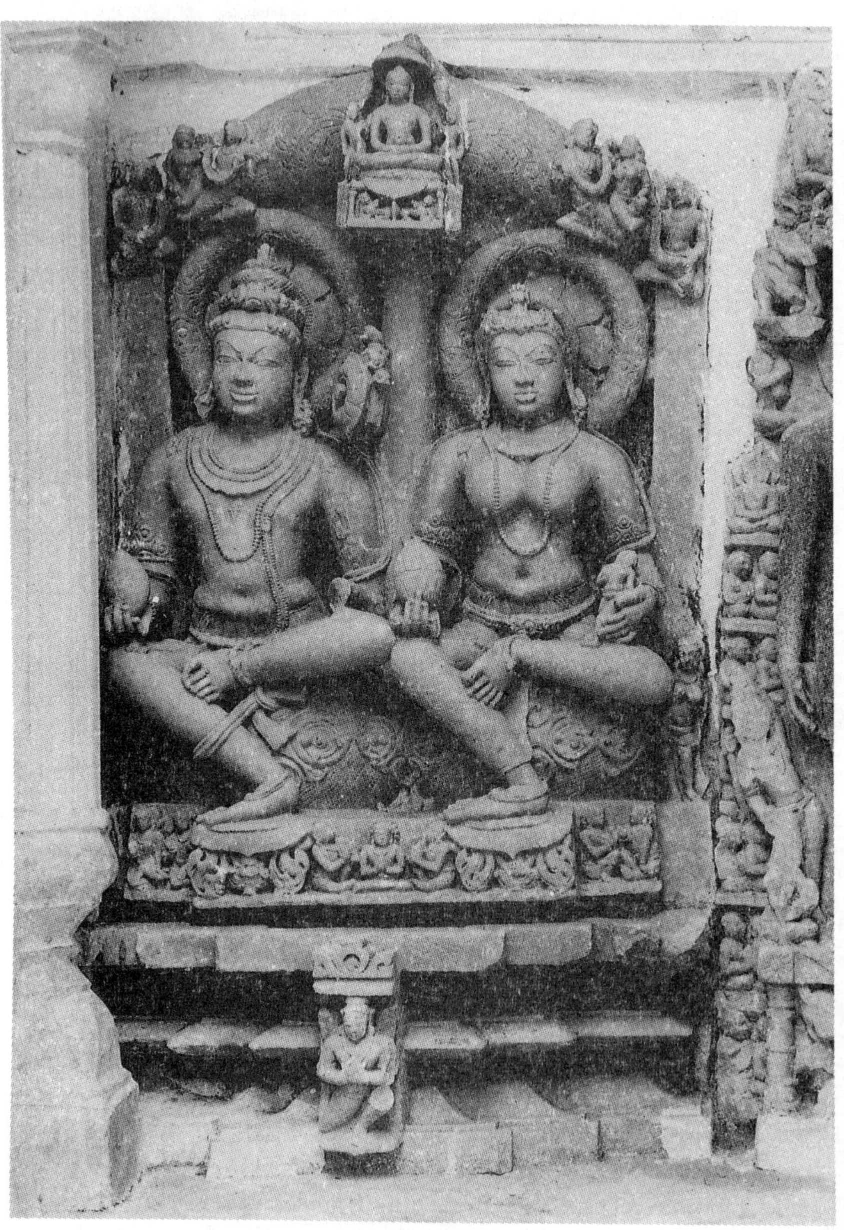

Photo 13. Yaksha couple, Shantinatha Jain complex

provided with cushions, and sheltered by an umbrella, the symbol of (spiritual) sovereignty. They are attended by flywhisk bearers. There is an elaborate pantheon, an assembly of celestial beings, surrounding the motionless figures of the Jina.

Yakshas and **Yakshis:** Jina images are only objects of meditation and no earthly rewards are expected from their veneration. It is the Yakshas and Yakshis, associated with the each of the Jinas as subsidiary figures, who fulfil the worldly needs of the devotees. They are depicted as richly adorned, and smaller in size than the Jina whom they serve. At Khajuraho, the images of Chakreshvari, Ambika, and Padmavati, the Yakshis of Adinatha, Neminatha, and Parshvanatha respectively, are found in large numbers. Chakreshvari is found at the centre of door lintels of the temples. Images of Chakreshvari depict her as a counterpart of the Hindu goddess Vaishnavi. She holds a discus (chakra) in her hand and rides the mythical bird, the Garuda. The Yakshi Ambika, shaded under a mango tree, holds a child and a bunch of mangos. Padmavati is distinguished by a snake over her head. Among the Yakshas, Sarvanubhuti (Kubera) and Gomukha have several representations at Khajuraho.

The Yaksha couple with a child, also called 'Parents of Jina', sit below a tree, surmounted by the figure of a Jina. This sacred pair seems to have been elevated to independent niches in the Jain temples, as can be seen from several such representations at Khajuraho. One such pair, now preserved in the Shantinatha temple, is among the most impressive sculptures of Khajuraho [**Ph. 13**].

S I X

The Monuments

Twenty-five temples survive today at Khajuraho. For convenience's sake, they are divided into three groups: 1) the western, near the Shivasagar tank, 2) the eastern, near the Khajursagar tank (Ninora Tal) and the Khajuraho village, 3) the southern, near the Khudar rivulet [see **Fig. XII**]. The remains of a large temple have recently been excavated by the Archaeological Survey of India in the southern area.

The Western Group

The most important and magnificent temples of Khajuraho, built by the royalty, are situated in the western group. They are now within an enclosure and a garden maintained by the Archaeological Survey of India. The temples are open to the public from sunrise to sunset and tickets cost a nominal amount. They are described below, as they appear, in clock-wise order.

Devi

This small structure faces the Lakshmana temple. It now contains an image of the goddess Brahmani, but originally it housed Vishnu's mount Garuda, the solar bird.

Varaha (Boar)

Facing west and in front of the Lakshmana temple, the Varaha sanctuary is an open pavilion with a pyramidal roof. It enshrines India's most powerful icon of Varaha, the third incarnation of Vishnu. Here he is portrayed as Yajna-Varaha, in animal form [Ph.14]. In Puranic myth, Vishnu as the Boar enters the primeval waters and lifts the Earth goddess from the nether region. The massive Boar, measuring 2.66 m. by 1.75 m., is carved out of a single piece of solid yellow sandstone. It is canopied by an exquisite lotus ceiling. This magnificent sculpture in the round is positioned in the centre of the shrine with space for devotees to walk around it in a circumambulation rite.

The divine animal carries on its body more than 675 miniature figures in twelve neatly carved rows. These figures depict all the important divinities of the Hindu pantheon, including Ganesha,

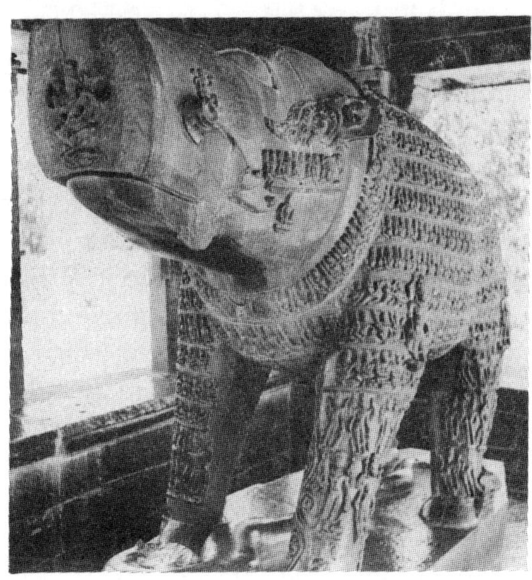

Photo 14. Varaha, the Boar incarnation of Vishnu

the seven Mothers, the seven sages, the eight Guardians of Space, the nine planetary divinities, the river goddesses, the seas, the Rudras, and the different forms of Vishnu. In fact, the Boar represents the cosmic form, Vishvarupa, embodying all beings. There was also an image of the Earth Goddess, which is now missing. Today, only her feet can be seen attached to the pedestal. In 1838, Captain T. S. Burt, the first Englishman to see and write on this fabulous Boar, tried hard to look for the lost image of the Goddess, but in vain.

The Varaha image dates to about AD 950 and was possibly installed by the Chandella king Yashovarman as a celebration of victory over his Pratihara overlord. There is a political metaphor implied in the installation of the Boar. Just as the Boar rescued the Earth goddess on the celestial level, the king saved her from the enemy on a more terrestrial level.

Lakshmana

This is one of the most refined and well-planned temples, not only in Khajuraho but in all of India [**Ph. 15**]. It enshrines an esoteric form of Vishnu called Vaikuntha. Major Cunningham, on his first visit to the temple in 1864, reported seeing this majestic image 1.3 m. (4 ft.) high with three faces of the Lion, Man, and Boar. The temple was affiliated to the Vaishnavite Pancharatra sect of the Kashmir school, which worshipped Vishnu in this composite form. The temple's inscription (now fixed in the porch) states that King Yashovarman built this splendid temple to house the Vaikuntha image that he acquired from his overlord, the Pratihara king, who in turn had got it from the ruler of Chamba region. The temple was consecrated by his son Dhangadeva in AD 954.

The Lakshmana temple is a five-shrined or panchayatana complex and stands in the centre of a high platform along with its four subsidiary shrines in the corners. All along the platform, a continuous sculptural frieze depicts scenes of everyday life: a royal hunt, battle, traders, dancers and musicians, dancer conversing with a religious teacher [see **Ph. 7**], and elixir preparation amidst an orgy. This is the only temple of Khajuraho which preserves sculptural panels on the platform.

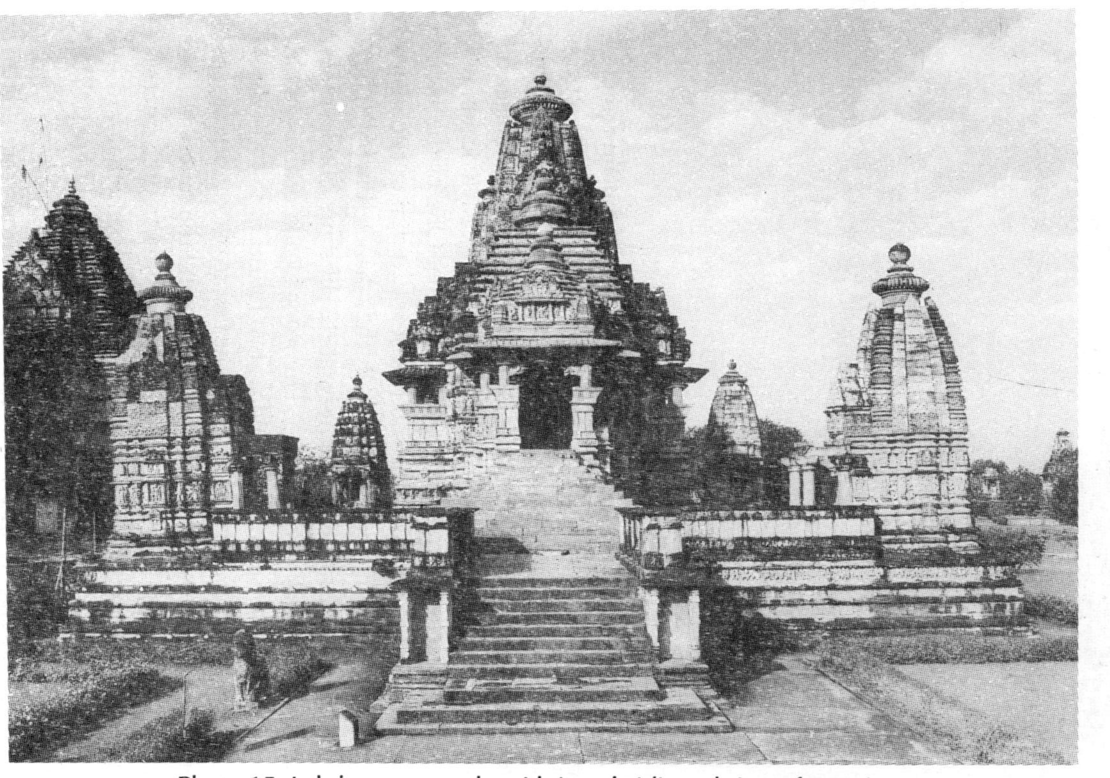

Photo 15. Lakshmana temple with its subsidiary shrines, front view

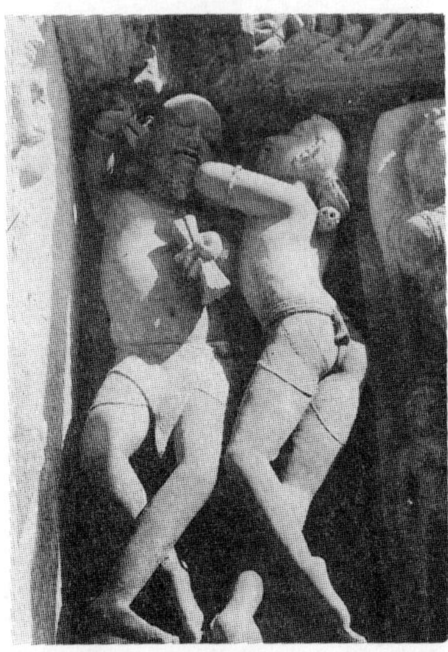

Photo 16. Male devotees dancing to the beat of castanets, Lakshmana temple

After climbing a few steps, one approaches the main temple. Its exterior wall is divided into two zones of sculptures depicting graceful apsaras, snake goddesses, griffins, and couples in the recesses. The upper zone, on its buttresses, carries the images of the different forms of Vishnu [see **Ph. 5**], while Shiva occupies a position on the buttresses of the lower zone. One of the more noteworthy sculptures on the south-east side is that of two males ecstatically dancing with castanets in their hands [**Ph.16**]. They are not homosexuals, as erroneously labeled by some, but devotees engrossed in Bhakti (devotion). The front façade of the temple has an image of the Sun god holding two lotuses.

The architect of this temple was the first to place erotic groups on the juncture wall of the mahamandapa and the sanctum. In a kind of visual pun, he has put the conjoint figures on this architectural juncture. Other puns have also been employed by him, the details of which I have worked out in my book, *The Religious Imagery of Khajuraho*.

One enters the interior of the temple through an arched gateway (torana), adorned with makaras. The brackets-pillars of the mahamandapa have figures of apsaras alternating with vyalas. The temple has an interesting sanctum doorway [**Ph.17, Fig. VII**].

This is the only temple in Khajuraho that depicts the avataras of Vishnu on its jambs, pairing Matsya (Fish), Varaha, and Vamana on the left jamb with Kurma (Tortoise), Narasimha, and Parashurama on the right jamb. The centre of the lintel is presided over by the goddess Lakshmi.

While one circumambulates the sanctum, one can see images of Vishnu's incarnations in the three cardinal niches of the walls: Varaha in the south, Narasimha in the west, and Hayagriva (Horse-necked one) in the north. In the upper western niche [**Ph.18**], Vishnu-Narayana can be seen amidst his devotees at Svetadvipa, a mythic island mentioned in the *Mahabharata* (Shanti Parva). The three placid scenes of Vishnu-Narayana discoursing with the sages are interspersed with twelve panels depicting Krishna slaying or subduing demons [see **Figs. V, VIII**].

Goddesses are also represented in this temple. Sculptures of Lakshmi, Sarasvati, Mahishasuramardini, Durga-Kshemankari with two lions, Tripura in meditation posture, and others are found in the niches of the sanctum and the mahamandapa.

The planetary divinities (Grahas) play an important part in the iconography of the Vaikuntha temple. In the interior of the temple they are represented on the door lintel of the sanctum, while on the exterior, their handsome figures are placed around the temple in all niches of the plinth. The architect has presented the temple as Mount Meru, the centre of the universe, around which the planetary divinities revolve.

Kandariya Mahadeva

One of the greatest monuments in India [**Ph.19**], this cave-like temple gets its name from the word *kandara* (cave). This is the tallest temple at Khajuraho, with a height of 30.5 m. It was possibly built by King Vidyadhara, in about AD 1030, after his successful combat with Mahmud of Ghazni.

A series of steps lead one to a high platform and then through an exquisite makara torana to the temple's interior. Walking through the porch and intricately decorated halls, one comes to the vestibule (antarala) and can have darshana (visual perception)

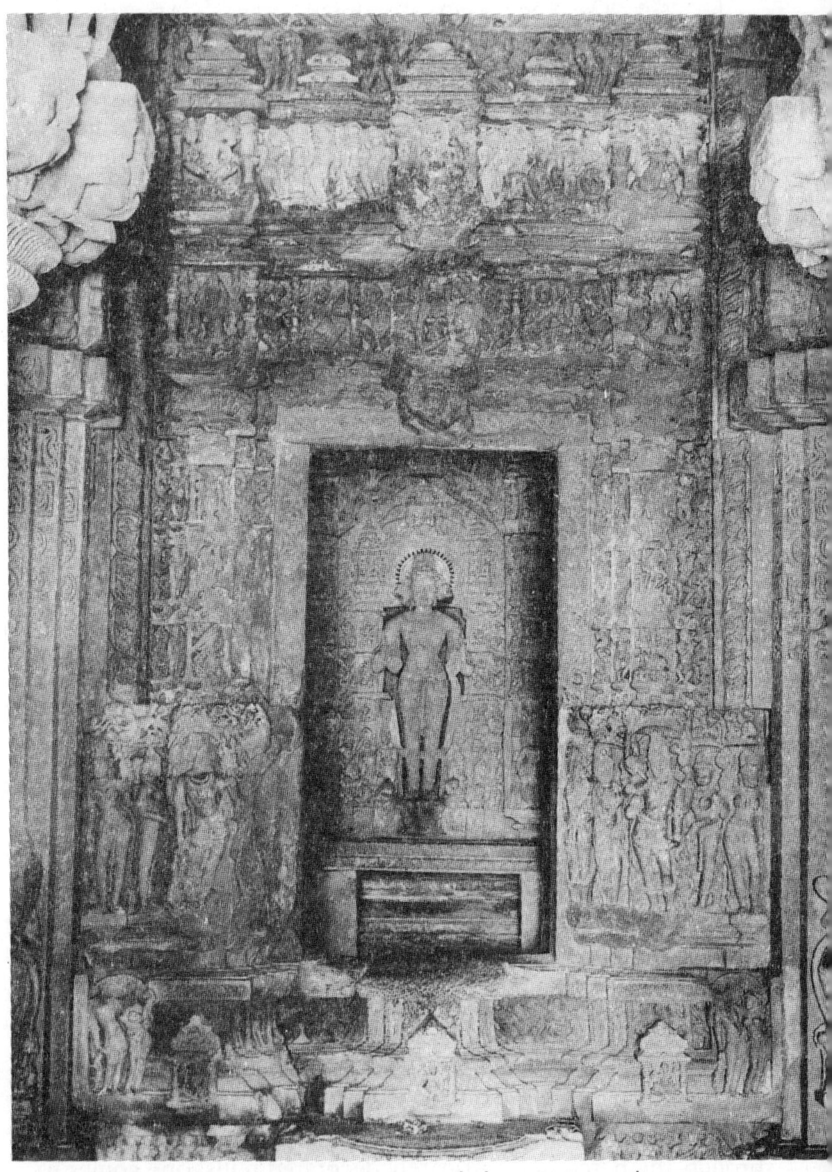

Photo 17. Vaikuntha image and the sanctum doorway, Lakshmana temple

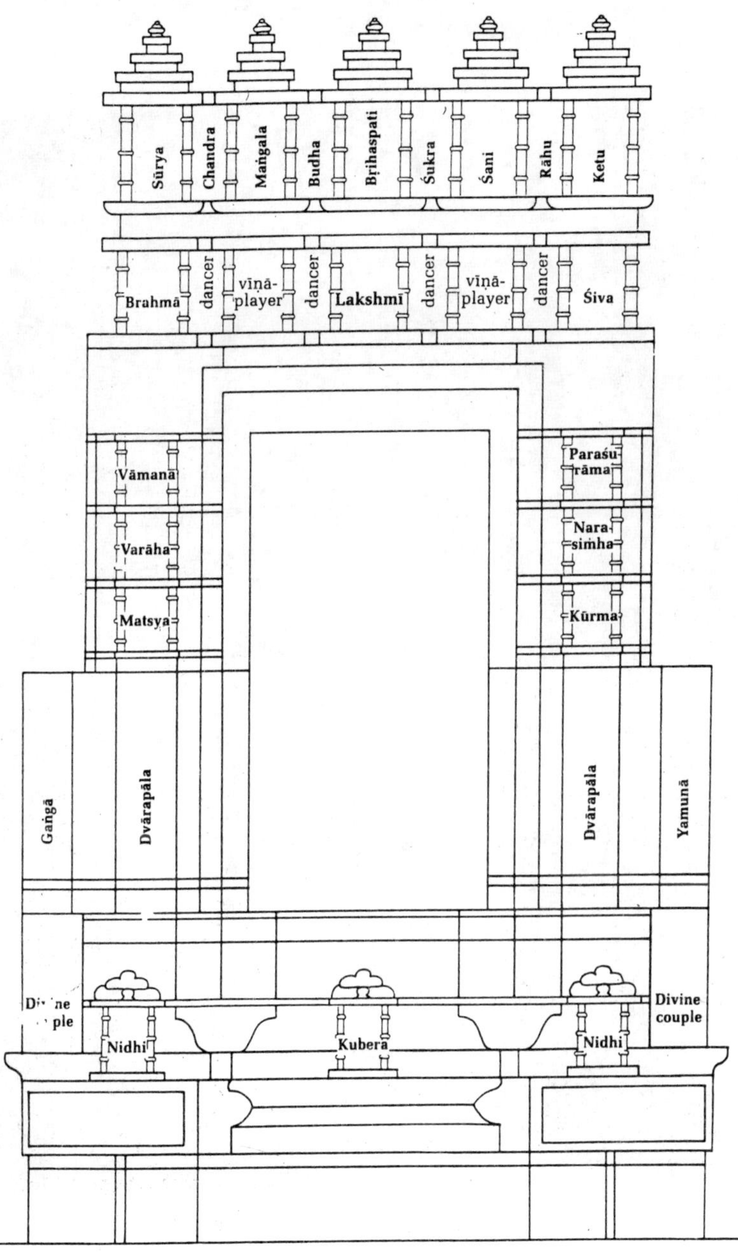

Fig. VII. Door divinities, sanctum, Lakshmana temple

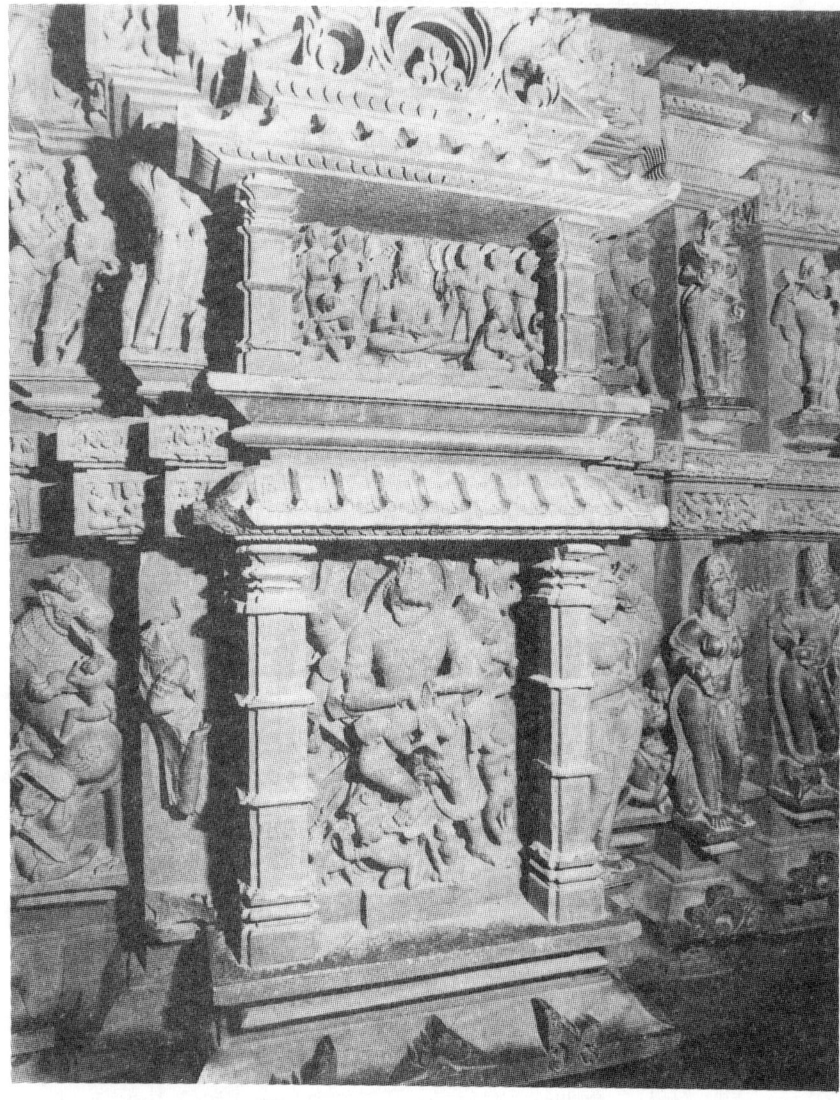

Photo 18. Narasimha and Vishnu-Narayana in the cardinal niches, and surasundaris on projections, sanctum wall, Lakshmana temple

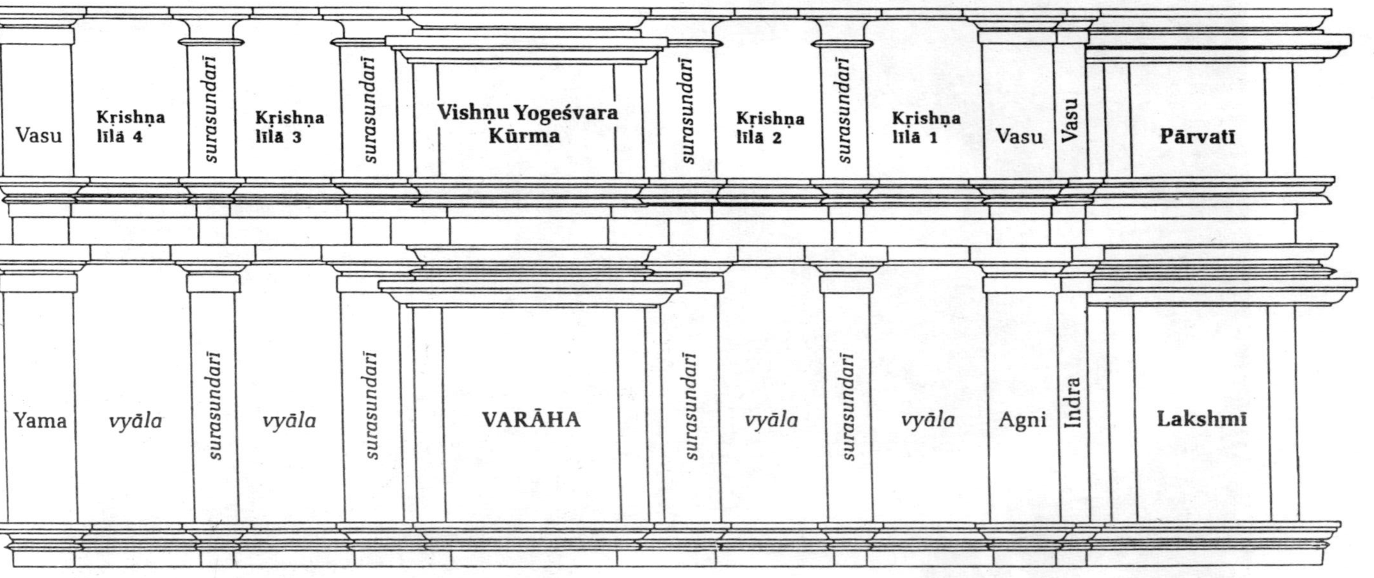

Fig. VIII. Arrangements of images, south elevation, sanctum, Lakshmana temple

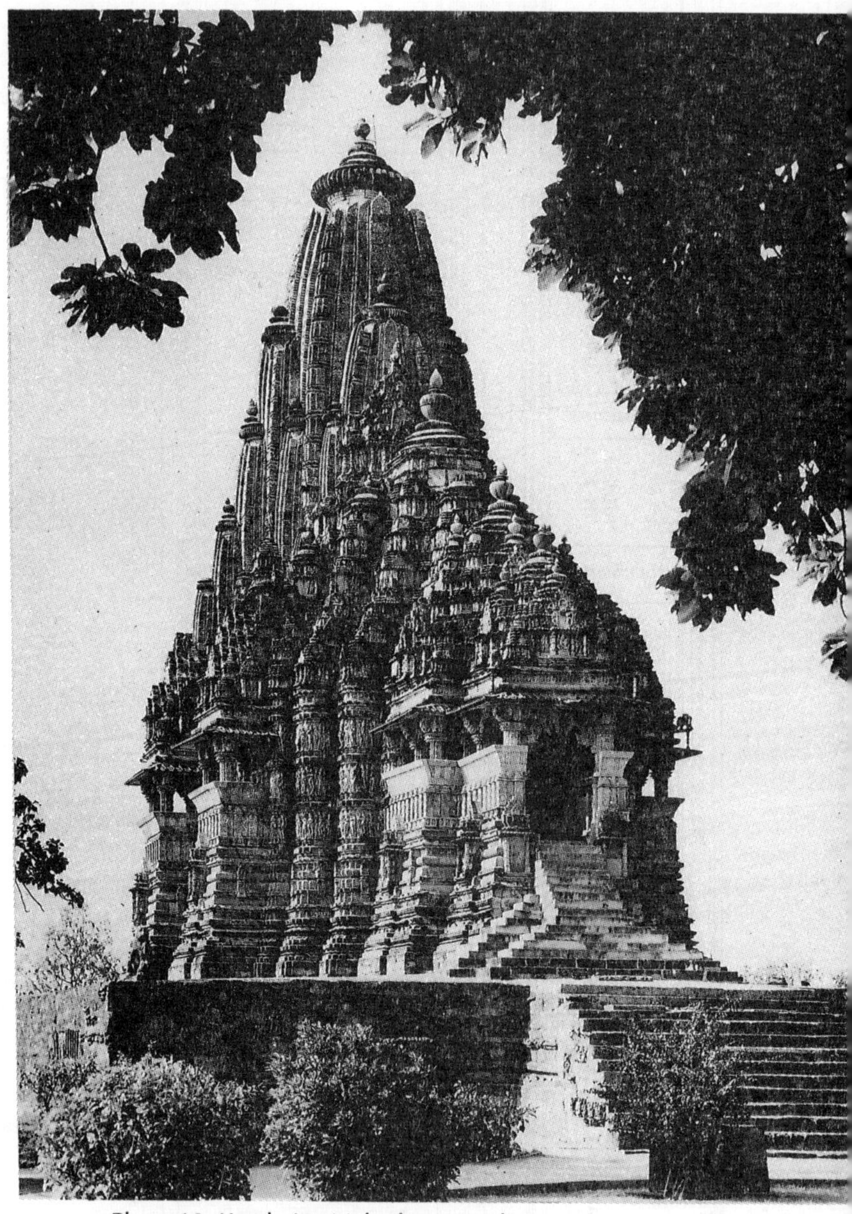

Photo 19. Kandariya Mahadeva temple

of the marble linga, placed exactly in the centre of the cella. One can then walk in the ambulatory around the sanctum in a clockwise direction.

The architect of the temple has presented a well-planned iconic scheme. In a niche of the large hall there is a unique four-footed (*chatushpada*) Sadashiva image. Sadashiva, considered to be the 'unmanifest-manifest' aspect of the Supreme Shiva, is pivotal to the Shaivite religious system. His four feet refer to the four parts (padas) of the Shaiva system that the builders of the temple followed. In the three cardinal niches of the sanctum wall are depicted Shiva's manifestations (*lila-murtis*): 1) subduer of the blind demon Andhaka, 2) the cosmic dancer Natesha, and 3) Tripurantaka, destroying the three demon cities.

On the exterior wall of the temple are three bands of sculpture representing apsaras, griffins, images of Shiva, Dikpalas, and snake goddesses in corners where rain water flows. Alexander Cunningham counted 646 figures on the exterior of this temple and 226 figures on its interior. The famous erotic groups are placed on the juncture of the big hall and the sanctum, which corresponds to the wall portion between the two balconies [see **Ph. 9**].

There is a unique counter-circumambulatory arrangement of the images of the seven Matrikas (Mothers), along with Ganesha and Shiva-Virabhadra, in the principal niches of the basal storey [**Fig. IX**]. The devotee, when circumambulating the temple, first sees Ganesha, then the seventh Matrika Chamunda. He meets with the first Matrika, Brahmani, only on completion of the round. This placement of the Matrikas could be explained on the grounds that the Matrikas themselves are circumambulating the abode of Shiva. Led by Virabhadra, followed by Ganesha, they encircle the temple forming a protective mandala (circle) around it. The architect has presented the Matrikas as if they are dancing around Shiva's abode [**Ph. 20**].

The Kandariya Mahadeva has been highly praised by art historians and connoisseurs for the superb harmony of the graded proportions of its various component units along with their

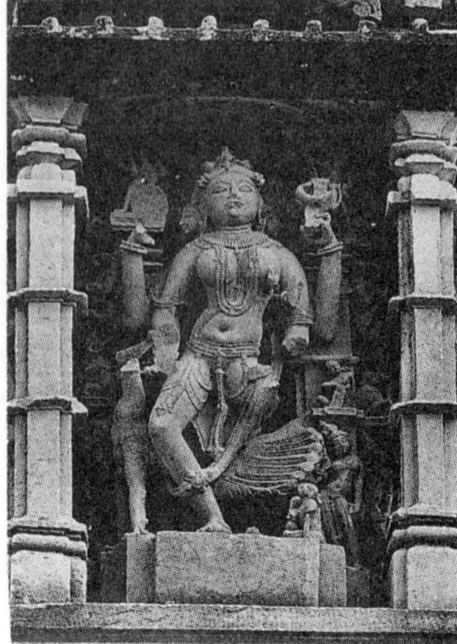

Photo 20. Dancing Matrika Kaumari, basal niche, Kandariya Mahadeva temple

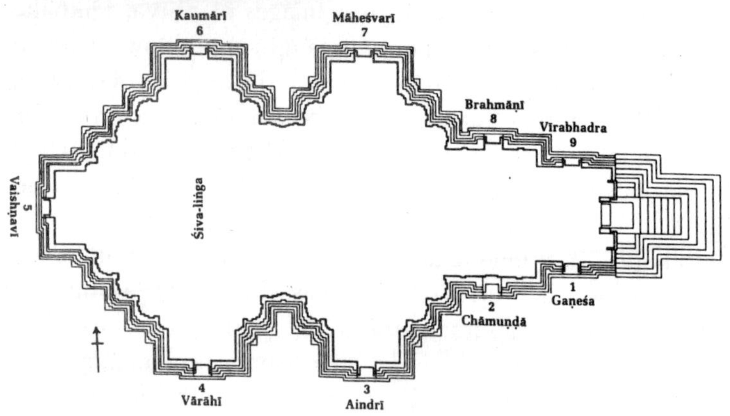

Fig. IX. Placement of Matrikas in the basal niches, Kandariya Mahadeva temple

superstructures. The spire of the sanctum has a series of graded replicas of itself, which cluster around the central peak and create the effect of a mountain range. In the soft evening light one can experience the rhythm of the ascent and descent of its mini-spires, leading the eye upwards to the summit. Exactly below the highest point of the spire is positioned the Shiva-linga, the 'Primordial Pillar of the Universe', (as a Chandella inscription calls the linga), in the dark womb-house or sanctum.

Mahadeva

On the same platform as the Kandariya Mahadeva, towards its north, lies this partially preserved structure, now called Mahadeva. It houses an important sculpture of a Lion and a Warrior, a favourite theme in Chandella and other Rajput art.

Devi Jagadamba

This temple, to the north of the Kandariya Mahadeva and on the same platform, was originally dedicated to Vishnu. This fact is known from the central image of this god on the door lintel of its sanctum. The original affiliation to Vishnu is also supported by the iconography of images in the cardinal niches of the temple. Now, however, the temple houses an image of the Devi (Goddess), who is worshipped by the local people on festive occasions. The *yajna kunda* for rituals in the centre of the hall was added by the Maharaja of Chhatarpur in the mid-nineteenth century.

The temple is famous for the graceful figure sculptures [**Ph. 21**] on its exterior wall—mithunas, apsaras, vyalas, and images of deities. Cunningham found the sculptures on the smaller row

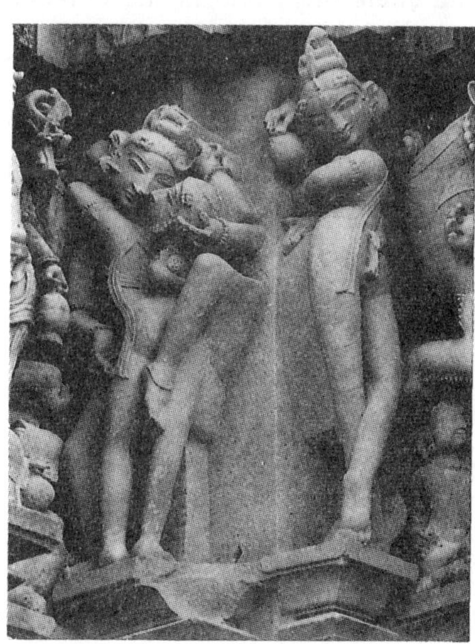

Photo 21. *Apsara,* and *mithuna,* exterior wall, Devi Jagadamba temple

to be highly indecent. The temple was built between AD 1000–1025.

Chitragupta

The only Surya (Sun) temple on this site, built between AD 1000–1025, the Chitragupta is situated to the north of the Devi Jagadamba, and in the north-west corner of the enclosure of the western group of temples. The icon of Surya, 2.13 m. (7 ft.) tall, stands equipoised in samabhanga. He wears an armoured coat and boots in the style of a northerner. The statue of one time held two lotus flowers, which are now broken. Seven horses pull his chariot. The centre of the door lintel of the sanctum is presided over by a composite image of Surya-Brahma.

The exterior of the temple is adorned with two bands of sculpture with beautiful apsaras, mithunas, vyalas, and deities. The uppermost smaller row has erotic figures and teacher-disciple groups. More than seventy ascetic figures are carved on the balcony panels (kakshasana) of this, just as on the Devi Jagadamba temple. A scene showing sculptors at work is carved on the plinth. There is an interesting iconographic form of the eleven-headed Vishnu in the niche of the south wall.

Chopra Tank

A little distance away from the Chitragupta temple, outside the fence of the western group of temples, is a small water tank, called the Chopra tank. It is a three-storeyed stepped tank. Its construction near the temple of Surya, associated with the healing of diseases, is noteworthy.

Parvati

Walking through the garden towards the east from the Chitragupta, one comes to the Parvati temple. This is a small shrine, heavily restored. It now houses an image of the goddess Parvati standing on an iguana (godha), but the sanctum door has a Vishnu in the centre.

Vishvanatha

One of the three grand temples at Khajuraho—the other two being the Lakshmana and the Kandariya—the Vishvanatha [see **Ph. 2**] was built by the powerful King Dhangadeva and consecrated in AD 999. It has a long inscription stating that Dhangadeva installed an emerald linga, along with a stone one. The temple was then known as the Marakateshvara, the Lord of the Emerald Linga. This precious linga was already missing in 1864, when Cunningham visited the temple.

Importantly, the inscription of this temple preserves the name of its architect, Sutradhara Chhichchha, who was well-versed in the architectural tradition of Vishvakarma.

It is also significant that this is the only temple at Khajuraho that has its Nandi-mandapa or pavilion for the bull mount of Shiva intact. A magnificent Nandi sits facing the temple.

Originally the Vishvanatha temple was five-shrined (panchayatana) like the Lakshmana, but now only two subsidiary shrines survive. It is a sandhara temple with an inner ambulatory. Graceful apsaras decorate the pilasters and the sanctum wall in the interior of the temple. One of Khajuraho's earlier representations of the theme of the apsara with a scorpion [see **Ph. 8**] can be found on the west wall of the sanctum. The main niches of the wall contain Shiva's manifestations: Andhakantaka subduing the blind demon, Natesha (now mutilated) dancing in the western light, and Ardhanari.

Other beautiful figures, arranged in three rows, adorn the exterior walls [see **Ph. 3**]. As in the other sandhara temples of Khajuraho, here too erotic groups are placed on the juncture of the mahamandapa and the sanctum. There are several figures of religious teachers on the plinth as well as on the lintel of the sanctum door.

The architect of this temple, Chhichchha, was apparently the first to place the seven Matrikas, in a peculiar counter circumambulatory manner on the exterior plinth. This placement was later adopted by the architect of the Kandariya Mahadeva.

Statue of Bhairava

Outside the fenced enclosure, on the way to the Matangeshvara temple and on one's right, under a tree, is a colossal statue of Bhairava, 1.98 m. (6.5 ft.) high. It is coated with red lead and is still worshipped today. Though he has raised curls associated with fierce deities, this Bhairava stands gracefully holding a cup, a lotus stalk and a staff. Stylistically, the image belongs to the early-tenth century. In 1865, Cunningham wrote that the statue was found while digging for stones to build a cenotaph for Pratap Singh, Maharaja of Chhatarpur.

Matangeshvara

The main temple in Khajuraho that is still used for worship, the Matangeshvara stands outside the fenced enclosure, on the south of the Lakshmana temple, and close to the bank of the Shivasagar tank. The Matangeshvara or the Mrityunjaya Mahadeva (Conquerer of Death) temple has one of the largest lingas in India—2.53 m. (8.3 ft.) high and more than one meter in diameter. A similar huge linga from almost the same period is also found at Bhojpur, in the vicinity of Bhopal. The roof of the Matangeshvara temple is pyramidal in structure and there is no sculptural decoration. This temple is dated to c. AD 1000 by architectural historians. During Shivaratri, a festival sacred to Shiva, devotees bathe in the Shivsagar tank and then proceed with a water pot to the Matangeshvara temple for worship.

Chausath Yogini

Walking along the Shivsagar tank and through the fields towards the south-west, one arrives at this unique open-air sanctuary [**Ph. 22**] situated away from the main group of temples. It was dedicated to the Chausath (sixty-four) Yoginis, manifestations of the Great Goddess. Unlike the other temples at Khajuraho, which are made of fine sandstone, this temple was constructed with granite blocks. It is considered by scholars to be one of the earliest shrines at Khajuraho, and has been dated to c. AD 900. This is the only shrine at the site that is aligned not east–west, but is oriented to the north-east [**Fig. X**].

The sanctuary, erected on a low rocky mount, consists of sixty-seven cells, of which one was larger than the rest. Each of the smaller cells used to house a Yogini, while the larger cell had an image of Durga-Mahishasuramardini, inscribed with the label 'Hinghalaja'. When Major Cunningham visited this sanctuary in 1865, he only found three images *in situ*— the goddess Hinghalaja in the principal cell and the two Matrikas Brahmani and Maheshvari in the cells flanking it. These three images are now at the Site Museum, as is the dancing Ganesha [see **Ph. 25**], who faced the Yogini sanctuary.

From the Yogini shrine one gets a picturesque view of the grand Kandariya Mahadeva temple.

Lalguan Mahadeva

This small shrine, dedicated to Shiva, is situated on the bank of the Lalguansagar lake, about half a kilometre from the Chausath Yogini sanctuary. Facing west, it is based on a simple plan, comprising a sanctum and a porch (now missing). The sanctum is covered with a pyramidal shikhara (partly preserved). The doorway is plain, with only a diamond design carved on the door-sill. This modest shrine belongs to a slightly later date than the Yogini temple—c. AD 900–925.

Shivsagar Tank

This water tank, called 'Sevamsagara' in inscriptions, is an important landmark in Khajuraho. The Shivsagar tank is possibly 'the large lake surrounded by towering temples' described by Ibn Battuta, the Arab traveller who visited Khajuraho in 1335. At the time of Captain Burt's visit in 1838, and Cunningham's in 1865, this water tank extended about three-quarters of a mile to the north, along the area behind the Matangeshvara, Lakshmana, and the Vishvanatha temples [**Fig. XI** site plan of 1865]. Referring to the Kandariya Mahadeva, Burt wrote, 'Near the water entrance to the temple, I found a lion or two', by which he meant the sculptures of the lions on the platform of the Kandariya temple. Cunningham mentions the Chitragupta to be on the west bank of the old bed of

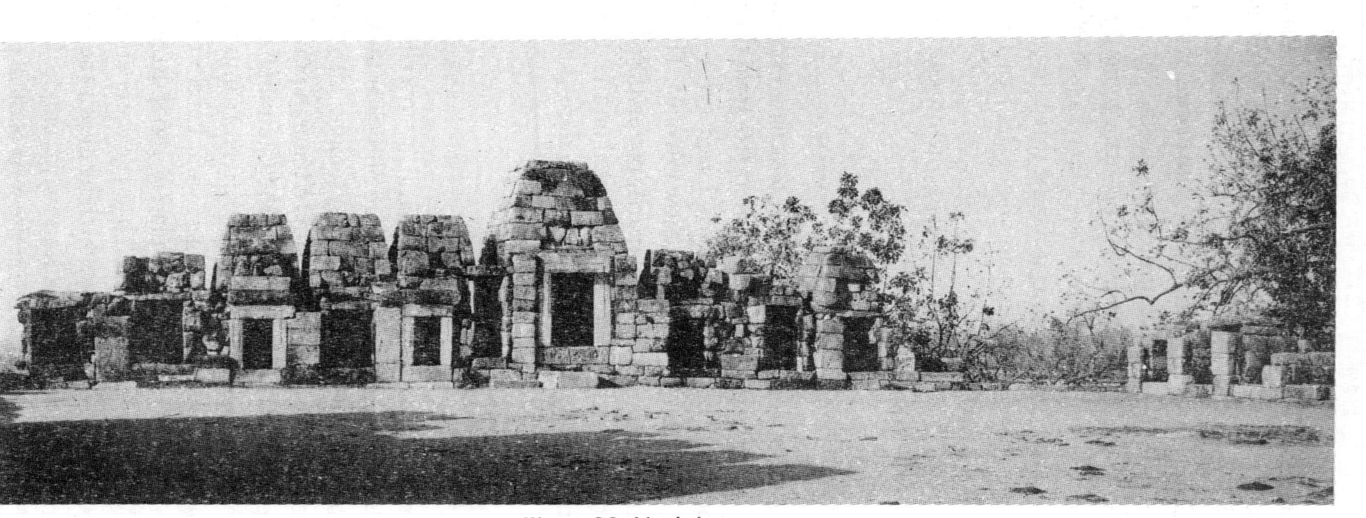

Photo 22. Yogini sanctuary

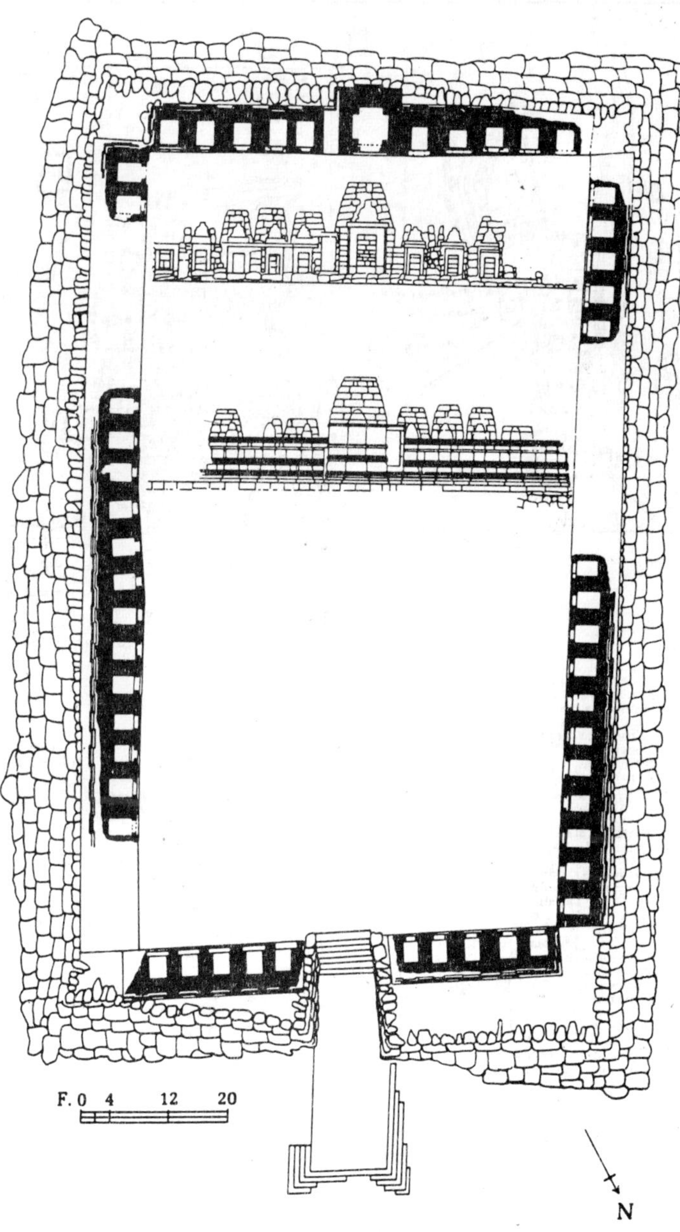

Fig. X. Yogini shrine, plan and part elevation

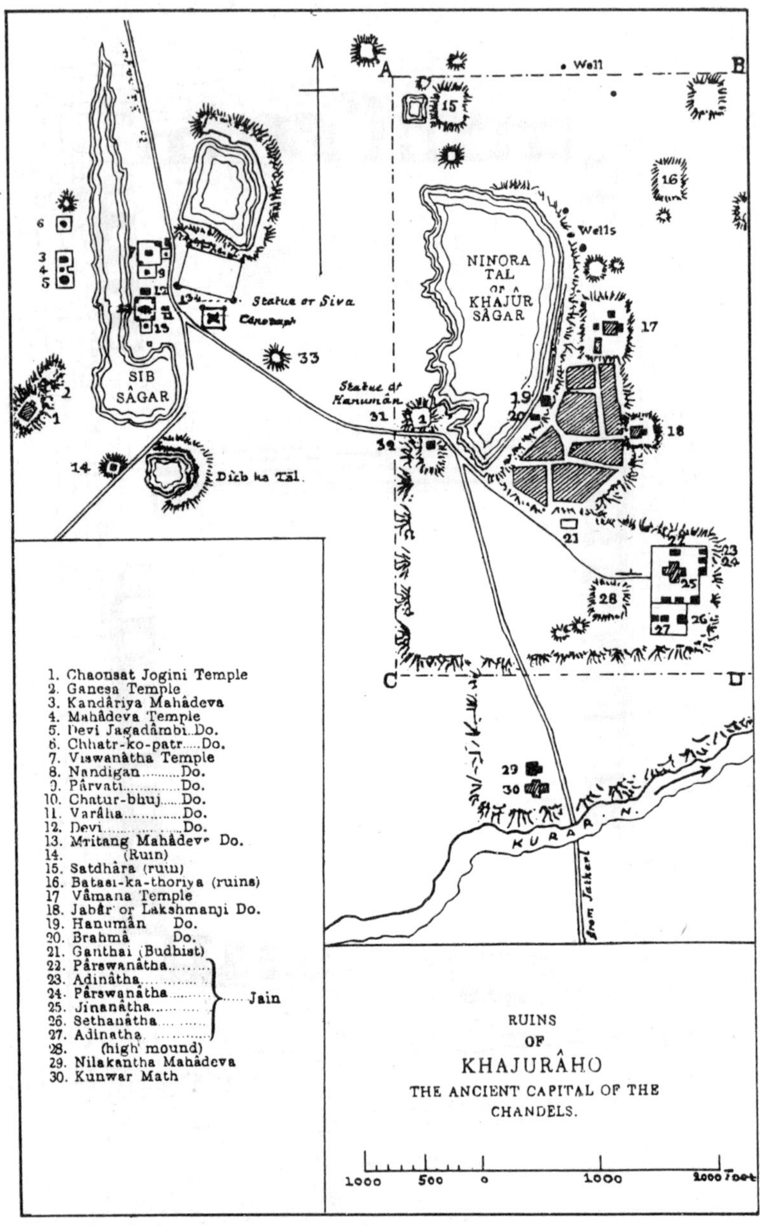

Fig. XI. Khajuraho site plan—1865, prepared by Major Alexander Cunningham

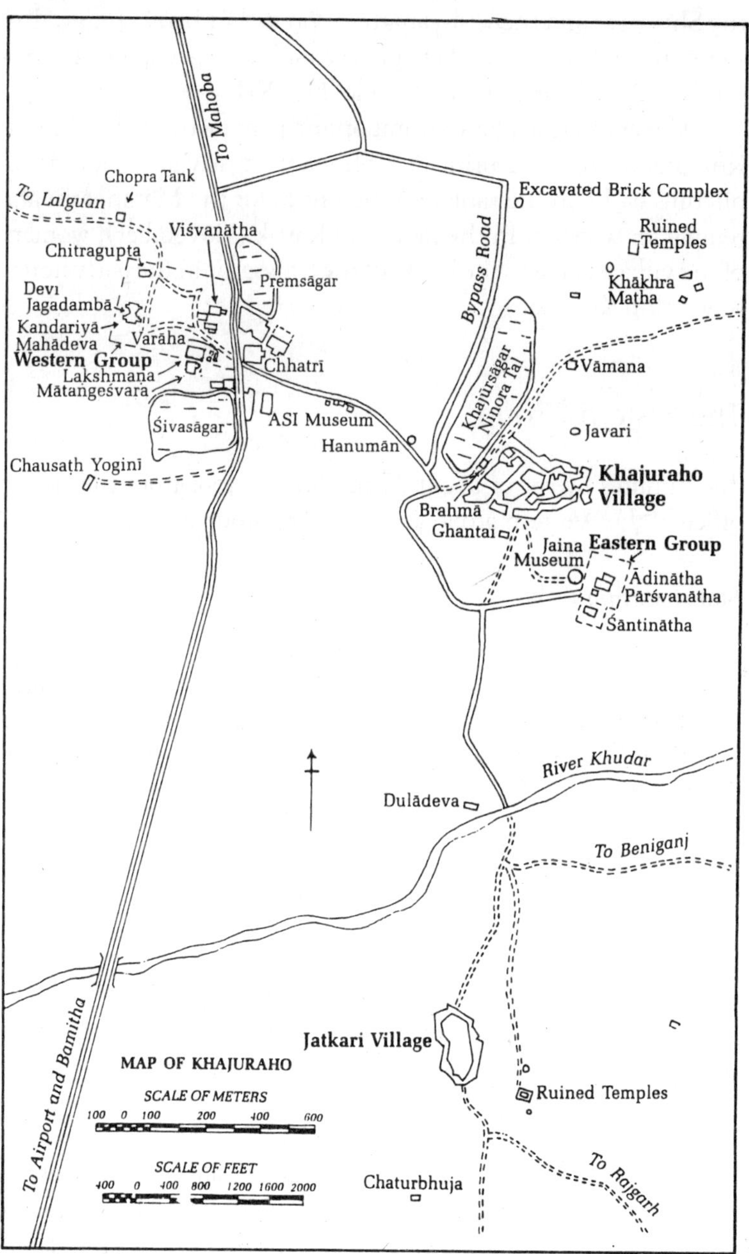

Fig. XII. Khajuraho site plan

the Shivsagar and the Vishvanatha as on its east bank. Today, this south–north bed has dried up and the tank only occupies the area south of the Matangeshvara temple [**Fig. XII**].

The Shivsagar plays an important part in the ritual life of Khajuraho village. During the Shivaratri festival, hundreds of pilgrims bathe in the tank and then head for the Matangeshvara temple for worship. In the month of Kartik (November), women of the village come to the banks of the Shivsagar in the early hours to worship Krishna.

The Eastern Group

Ten minutes by car or about 25 minutes on foot from the ticket office of the Western group is the Eastern group of temples.

Statue of Hanuman

On the way to the Jain temples is a recently built, white-washed shrine that shelters one of the earliest inscribed images of Hanuman in India. This 2.5 m. (8.2 ft.) high image of the monkey god, which is still worshipped today, is coated with red lead. It has a short dedicatory inscription dated AD 922.

Brahma

This temple is situated picturesquely on the banks of the Khajursagar tank with Khajuraho village as its backdrop. It presently shelters a four-faced Shiva-linga, because of which the temple was wrongly attributed to Brahma, who has four faces. But the temple was originally dedicated to Vishnu, for there is an image of Vishnu in the centre of its lintel. The temple is based on a simple plan, with a body of granite and a pyramidal spire made of sandstone. It does not have the usual sculptural adornment on its walls as do the other Khajuraho temples, but it has figures of the river goddesses Ganga and Yamuna on either side of the door. The temple has been dated at AD 925.

The Vishnu Temples: Vamana and Javari

The Vamana and the Javari temples are situated in the middle of a field. The Vamana, built between AD 1050 and 1075, enshrines a chubby icon of the Dwarf incarnation of Vishnu. This is an important temple as there are not many temples that are dedicated to this incarnation of Vishnu. Khajuraho, however, was a major centre for the worship of Vamana. A recently excavated brick complex to the north of the Vamana temple has yielded exquisite statues of Vamana.

The name 'Javari', given to the adjacent Vishnu shrine, is a local variation that derives from the 'javara' (millet) grown in the surrounding fields. This small temple was constructed between AD 1075 and 1100. It has an ornate torana (gateway).

Both these Vishnu temples have two bands of sculptures, with lovely apsaras and divinities on their walls. Incarnations of Vishnu are placed in cardinal niches of the temples.

Khajuraho Village

Nearby lies the village with white-washed houses and narrow lanes. On festivals like Divali (October–November), almost all the houses are decorated with auspicious floor paintings (rangoli) made from indigenous colours or rice flour. Some of the geometrical designs have been passed down from mother to daughter over centuries.

There is a goddess temple in the centre of the village, and another temple dedicated to Shiva, with some old images embedded in the wall. A Krishna temple is still used for regular worship. On festivals such as Navaratri, in honour of the Great Goddess Durga, the Goddess is invoked in several houses. On the ninth day of the festival, clay pots with sprouts of millet (javara) are placed on the roof of the village temple, or women carry these pots to the Yogini temple or Devi Jagadamba temple in the Western complex. In the month of Kartik (November), the village women worship Krishna daily, taking a small image with them to the banks of the Shivsagar tank. On the last day, they move out in a procession singing age-old songs.

In the by-lanes of the village are some interesting curio shops selling locally-manufactured metal objects. The village boys have started picking up different foreign languages such as English, German, French, Spanish, Italian, and Japanese. Now, even German and Spanish language classes are offered here. The village boys dream of earning their living as tourist guides or owning curio shops.

The Jain Temples

A group of Jain temples, protected within a modern compound wall, is situated to the south-east of Khajuraho village. A Jain Museum has been recently built near the entrance (see under **Museums**).

Parshvanatha

This largest of the Jain temples has beautiful figure sculptures on its exterior wall [Ph. 23]. It is a sandhara temple with an inner

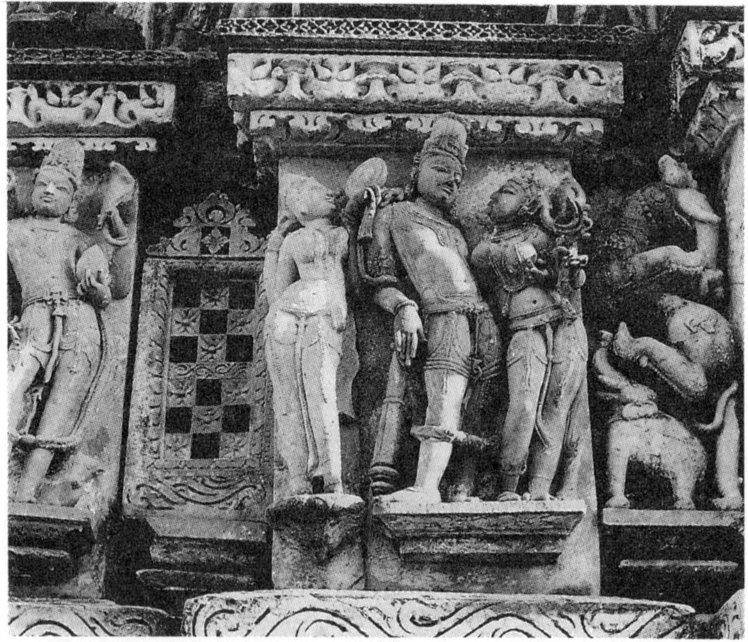

Photo 23. Figure sculpture on the wall, Parshvanatha temple

ambulatory and an oblong ground plan. Unlike other Khajuraho temples, this temple has no balconied openings but only perforated windows, and therefore have no void to relieve the monotony. The temple was built between AD 950 and 970, in the time of King Dhangadeva. It has an inscription mentioning a certain Pahila, who was respected by Dhangadeva. The temple was originally dedicated to Adinatha, the first Tirthankara, but the present image of Parshvanatha was installed in 1860, when some renovation work was undertaken.

Many fascinating figures of apsaras are found on the exterior wall of this temple. They are caught in the act of wearing an anklet, applying eye make-up, and writing a letter, among others. The temple has a rich variety of vyalas with faces of parrots, lions, elephants, and other creatures. Lively flying figures animate the upper zone of the wall.

It is still unclear why this Jain temple contains images of Krishna, Rama, Balarama, Vishnu, and Shiva on its exterior wall. The *kirita-mukuta*-wearing gatekeepers on the doorway represent the Jain Indra and Upendra, and are not to be misunderstood as figures of Vishnu. The Jain goddesses are seen in the niches of the juncture wall. A sculpture of the Parents of Jina is placed in the mahamandapa. The door lintel of the sanctum has figures of the Jinas, while that of the main hall contains the Yakshi Chakreshvari, the guardian Yakshi of Adinatha.

Adinatha

This temple, with only its sanctum and vestibule still remaining, is situated to the north of the Parshvanatha shrine. It is a single-spired temple and the crisp decoration of chaitya-arch designs on the spire creates an interesting light-and-shade effect. On the walls of the temple, there are beautiful apsaras in classical dance postures. They are decked with ornaments in their hair, ears, arms, and waist. There are numerous Jain Yakshis—Padmavati, Chakreshvari, Ambika, Manasi, and others in the niches of the walls. The door lintel bears the sixteen auspicious symbols that Jina's mother dreamt of at the time of conception.

Shantinatha Temple Complex

This is a principal site of Jain worship at Khajuraho. The temple complex, with several small shrines, consists of components of older temples and sculptures from 1027 and earlier. These were built into a composite structure about a hundred years ago. The main sanctuary houses a 4.3 m. (14 ft.) polished icon of a standing Shantinatha bearing a dedicatory inscription of AD 1027. An interesting twelfth century sculpture of a dancing Kshetrapala is present at the entrance to the sanctuary.

There is a marvellous sculpture of a Yaksha couple [see **Ph. 13**] on the right as one enters the complex. Stylistically, it can be dated to the early tenth century, but it has been placed at this site only within the last 80 years.

Ghantai

The approach to this temple is through a lane in the southern part of the village. The surrounding area is rich in mounds and contains remains of ancient structures. This tenth century Jain monument is known by its local name because of the 'Ghanta' (bell) motifs on its pillars. Its ground plan is similar to that of the Parshvanatha temple, but its walls have collapsed, and only the pillars of its porch and hall have survived along with an ornate ceiling, lintel, and doorway. According to architecture historian Krishna Deva, its pillars are 'among the finest pillars of medieval India, known for their stately form, restrained ornamentation, and classical dignity'. The gatekeepers and river goddesses wear rich ornaments. If this shrine was well preserved, it would probably have been one of the grandest monuments of Khajuraho.

Cunningham found an inscribed Buddha image (now in the Museum) near the Ghantai and therefore took this for a Buddhist shrine. Later, however, he excavated numerous Jina images in and around this structure and concluded that it was a Jain shrine. Its dedication to the Jain Digambara faith can further be attested by the carving of the sixteen auspicious symbols of the dream of Jina's mother on the upper lintel. The centre of the main lintel represents the Jain goddess Chakreshvari riding a Garuda, which suggests that the shrine was dedicated to Adinatha.

The Southern Group

Duladeva

The Shiva temple, locally called Duladeva, stands near the Khuddar rivulet. Chronologically, this is the last of Khajuraho's great temples. It was possibly constructed by the powerful Chandella king Madanavarman, in about AD 1130. It displays a marked change from the earlier temples in its architectural and sculptural style in that its figures have sharp features and angular postures, and wear typical trefoil crowns and leg ornaments. The figures are also heavily ornamented. This style was prevalent in the Chandella domain even outside Khajuraho, at Jamsot in the Allahabad region.

The temple shows influences of Western Indian architectural traditions. Its sanctum was built as if by rotating a square round a central axis. Such a plan is not found in any of the earlier temples of Khajuraho. Its mahamandapa is large and octagonal, with a corbelled circular ceiling. It originally had twenty apsara brackets, grouped in bunches of two or three, as Krishna Deva reports. Now some of these are in the Site Museum [see **Ph. 6**]. Although these apsaras and the celestial musicians on the upper row of the wall are shown in dynamic movement, the iconic sculptures of this temple stand in stereotyped attitudes.

The Hindi name 'Duladeva', young bridegroom, refers to a local tribal myth of Dulhadeva who, like the corn spirit, is wedded and slain amidst marriage celebrations, as part of fertility rituals. The name must have been given to this temple in the post-Chandella period.

Chaturbhuja

Located at some distance from the main group of temples, south-west of the Jatkari village and near the airport, the Chaturbhuja temple should ideally be visited in the afternoon at around 4.30 pm, when its magnificent icon is lit by the rays of the setting sun. The temple faces west, unlike most of the Khajuraho temples, which are oriented to the east. The evening *puja* (worship) must have played an important part in this temple. Stylistically, it is datable to around AD 1100.

The temple has an image of Vishnu on its door lintel and houses in its specially built sunken sanctum one of the most majestic icons of northern India, a 2.75 m. (9 ft.) high statue of an unusual ascetic form of Vishnu [**Ph. 24**]. This charming god, with matted hair and ornaments, is chaturbhuja (four-armed), hence the name of the temple. His lower right hand (now broken) was possibly in a *varada* (boon-giving) gesture, while his upper right hand is in an *abhaya mudra* (gesture of fearlessness). The upper left hand carries a book along with a lotus stalk and the lower left possibly a water-pot or a conch shell (now broken).

It is difficult to agree with archaeologist R. Sengupta who believes that the image represents Shiva in his Dakshinamurti form, preaching knowledge. It was always the linga and not the image of Shiva that was worshipped in the centre of the sanctum in this period. The door-guardians with their *jata-mukuta* need not be the reason for the Shaivite affiliation of the temple, for guardians with similar features are present in other Vishnu temples at Khajuraho also. It is more probable that this benevolent god standing in a peculiar stance with his weight on the left foot resembles Krishna Yogeshvara, the lord of Yoga, or he could possibly be the ascetic god Narayana, associated with Pancharatra and Bhakti. The earlier Lakshmana (Vaikuntha) temple was also affiliated to the Pancharatra religious system.

The exterior of the temple has been much restored. In a northern niche is a rare image of the esoteric goddess Narasimhi, with a lion's face and a human body. Below is an image of Vishnu. Images of Ardhanarishvara and Surya are seen in the southern and eastern niches.

Excavated Bijamandala (Vaidyanatha) Temple

In March 1999, to mark the Khajuraho Millenium year, the Archaeological Survey began excavation of the Bijamandala mound

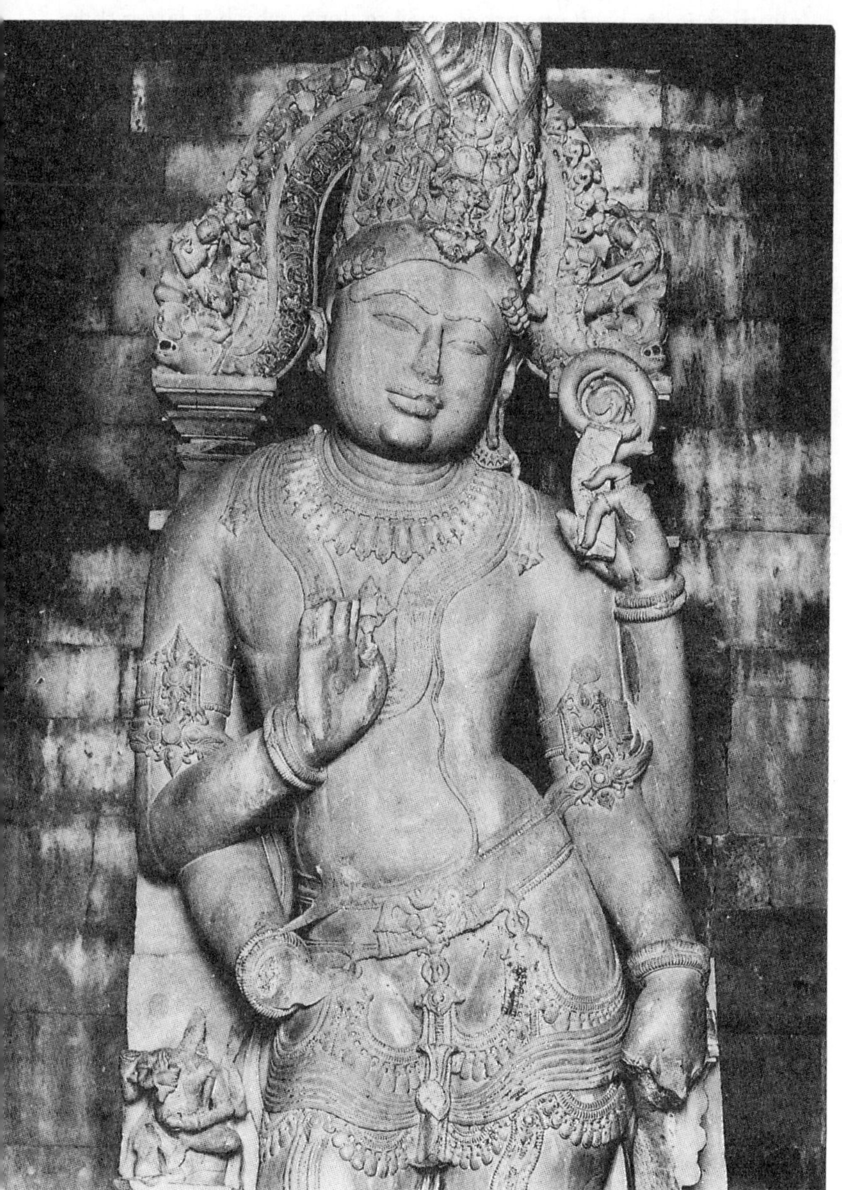

Photo 24. The unusual ascetic form of Vishnu, Chaturbhuja
temple

near the Jatkari village, not far from the Chaturbhuja temple. The plinth that has been unearthed is 34 m. long, which is larger than the 30 m. plinth of the Kandariya Mahadeva, so far the biggest temple at Khajuraho. This suggests that this excavated temple should be the largest at Khajuraho. The temple has an exquisite image of Sarasvati in a niche of its mandapa (now shifted to the Site Museum). Images of Brahma, Vishnu, Shiva as well as figures of apsaras and vyalas have been found. There is a small Jina figure in the sculptural relief of the plinth, which reminds one of the similar theme on the Vishvanatha and Devi Jagadamba temples of the western group. A stylistic study of the plinth mouldings suggests that the temple is pre-Kandariya Mahadeva, and nearer in date to the Devi Jagadamba temple (c. 1000–1025). It is likely to be the Vaidyanatha Shiva temple, built by Gahapati Kokkala, mentioned in his inscription of AD 1001. (*Epigraphia Indica*, Vol. I, pp. 147–8).

SEVEN

Museums

The Archaeological Museum, ASI

The Museum is situated opposite the Shivsagar tank, on the main road, not far from the Western group of temples. The advantage of seeing sculptures in the museum is that one can see them at eye level, as a result of which many details can be observed that would otherwise have been missed if the sculptures were seen high up in the dark halls of the temples.

The Museum shelters about a hundred representative stone sculptures from Khajuraho, ranging from between the tenth and twelfth centuries. They are arranged thematically into: 1) Shaivite and Shakta Gallery, 2) Vaishnavite Gallery, and the 3) Jain Gallery. There are also sculptures of miscellaneous subjects, including secular ones.

The entrance has superb door jambs with the river goddesses Ganga and Yamuna, and a lintel with Ardhanarishvara (Shiva androgyn) in the centre. It is one of the largest lintels found at the site and indicates the existence of a huge temple, bigger than the Kandariya Mahadeva, which once stood at Khajuraho.

As one enters, there is a handsome Ganesha, dancing gracefully to the beat of a drummer shown on his side [**Ph. 25**]. Originally, this tenth century image was spotted by Major Cunningham in front of the Yogini temple. In the same ante-chamber is the only image of the Buddha found in Khajuraho, discovered by Cunningham in the vicinity of the Ghantai temple. There is also an icon of Hari-Hara, combining the two gods Vishnu (Hari) and Shiva (Hara), standing in samabhanga. Nearby is an image of the sun god, accompanied by his retinue, shown standing on his chariot drawn by seven horses.

In the room on the right are miscellaneous sculptures. The sculpture of the Chandella king and queen performing a ritual [see **Ph. 1**] is among the few that show royal figures. The panel depicting sculptors at work is a rare depiction of artists at Khajuraho. Apsara-bracket figures are exhibited on the upper part of the wall.

In the Shaivite and Shakta Gallery is a unique inscribed image of a four-footed Sadashiva with six visible faces [see **Ph. 11**]. A colossal Parvati standing on an iguana was probably once the main icon of worship in a large temple. Other noteworthy sculptures are: Shiva as Ardhanarishvara, the Seven Matrikas dancing along with Virabhadra and Ganesha, and an image of Ganesha with his consort.

In the Vaishnavite Gallery, one should not miss the extraordinary sculpture of Vishnu, seated in *yogasana* and making a gesture of silence with his forefinger. There is also a four-faced composite image of standing Vaikuntha with the faces of a lion, a man, a boar, and a horse (at the back), an image of Varaha, with a boar's head and a human body, rescuing the Earth Goddess who is seated on his left arm, and a lintel depicting the incarnations of Vishnu.

The Jain Gallery has several well carved images of Tirthankaras: Adinatha [see **Ph. 12**], Kunthunatha, Parshvanatha, and Mahavira. There are interesting sculptures of the Yakshi Ambika standing under a mango tree, and the goddess Manovega with a horse mount on her pedestal. Most remarkable are the sculptures of the 'Parents of Jina', with a tiny figure of Jina carved on the stylized tree under which they are sitting.

The Museum is open from 10 am to 5 pm on all days except Fridays. The entry ticket to the Western group of temples is valid

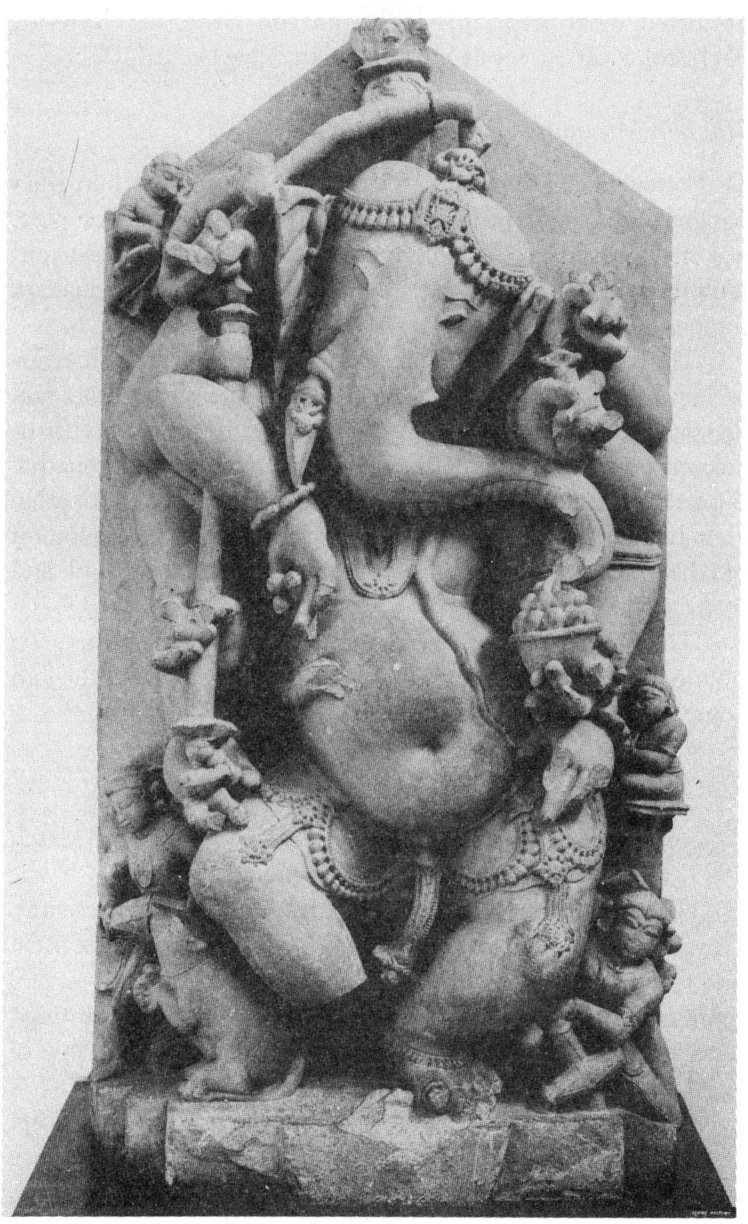

Photo 25. Dancing Ganesha, ASI Museum

for the Museum. Photography is only permitted to those who have obtained written permission from the Director General, Archaeological Survey of India, Janpath, New Delhi 110011.

The Jain Museum

This circular building, known as Sahu Shantiprasad Jain Kala Sangrahalaya, within the precincts of the Jain temple complex, was inaugurated in 1987. It houses more than a hundred Jain sculptures. At the entrance are two large ornamented makara toranas, arranged on both sides of the steps.

The Museum displays some noteworthy images of Tirthankaras, Jain Yakshis and Yakshas, Kshetrapalas, religious preceptors, and door jambs, door lintels, all found in Khajuraho. The images of Tirthankaras include those of Adinatha, Ajitanatha, Sambhavanatha, Suparshvanatha, Abhinandananatha, Vimalanatha, Shantinatha, Neminatha, Parshvanatha, and Mahavira. There are also sculptures of Chakreshvari, Padmavati, Ambika, Gandhari, Jvalamalini, and other goddesses.

The Museum is open every day, from 7 am to 6 pm. There is a nominal entrance fee. For photography, the main office in the Jain complex may be contacted.

The State Museum of Tribal and Folk Arts

This museum was inaugurated by the President of India on 8 March 1999, as part of the Khajuraho Millennium celebrations. It was established by the Directorate of Archaeology and Museums, Government of Madhya Pradesh, and houses a collection of tribal and folk artefacts from all over Madhya Pradesh. It has over 500 representative items of terracotta, metalcraft, woodcraft, paintings, jewellery, masks, and tattoos of different tribes and rural folk of this large and colourful state of India.

The Museum is open on all days from 12 noon to 8 pm except on Mondays and Government holidays. There is a nominal entrance fee. The Museum shop sells books and plaster casts including those of images from other museums in Madhya Pradesh.

Around Khajuraho

Khajuraho is situated in picturesque surroundings of forests, waterfalls, and historical monuments. There are some interesting spots on the banks of the Ken river, which rises from the Vindhya hills, flows in a northerly direction and joins the Yamuna river. Tourist cars, jeeps, and private buses are available for touring the sites around Khajuraho. Following are some of the sites that are worth visiting. The approximate distances mentioned are from Khajuraho:

Raneh Waterfalls: 20 km to the west, on the river Ken, with a stunning rock formation in a variety of colours.

Ken Gharial Sanctuary: 24 km further down the Raneh Falls, at the confluence of the Ken and Khudar rivers.

Benisagar Lake: 11 km; a waterspread of 7.7 sq km, and a dam on the river Khudar, on the road to Bamitha.

Mahoba: 65 km north of Khajuraho. One of the capitals of the Chandellas, Mahoba has temples built on islands in the lakes. The fourth Chandella ruler Rahilya constructed a large tank, called Rahilyasagar. The Kiratsagar lake is attributed by tradition to King

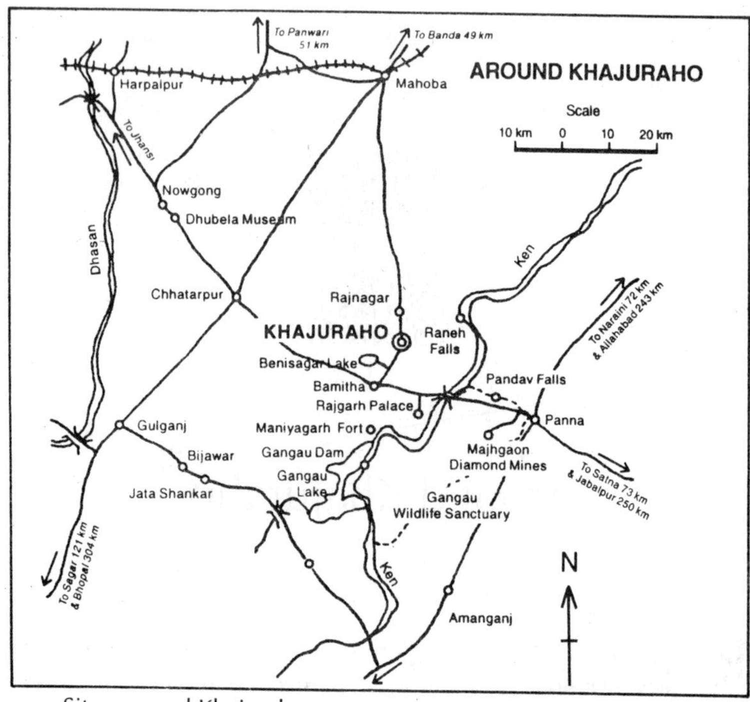

Sites around Khajuraho

Kirtivarman, and Madanasagar and a granite temple to King Madanavarman. The remains of the palace of King Paramardi, though later turned into a mosque, are believed to be located in the fort area.

Dhubela Museum: 57 km on the road from Khajuraho to Jhansi, near Nowgong. The Museum is housed within an old palace. It displays medieval sculptures from Shahdol and other neighbouring sites, and includes dynamic tenth and eleventh century Yogini images and some fine Jina icons. The Museum also has in its collection weapons, traditional garments, and other artefacts of the Bundela Rajput rulers. Not far from the Museum, on the banks of the Jagatsagar lake, are the remains of two eleventh century temples. The Museum is open on all days between 10 am and 5 pm except on Mondays and public holidays.

Rajgarh Palace: 25 km; at the foot of Maniyagadh hill. This fort-cum-palace was built by the Parmar rulers of Chhatarpur state in the middle of the nineteenth century.

Gangau Dam: 34 km; at the confluence of the Ken and Simri rivers, off the Bamitha–Panna road. The dam is surrounded by the Panna National Park and Gangau Sanctuary.

Panna National Park: 36 km on the Bamitha–Panna road, this park, spread over 540 sq. km along the eastern bank of the Ken river, is home to a variety of wild life including the spotted deer, boar, panther, and tiger. The best time to visit it is in winter. It is closed from June to October.

Pandav Waterfalls: 34 km, on a short diversion from the main Bamitha–Panna road, this is a spectacular site.

Gilles' Tree House and Ken River Lodge: Tree houses on the banks of the Ken river. Popular picnic spots. For more information and accommodation inquire at Raja Cafe, Khajuraho.

Panna: 46 km; a small historical town, capital of the Bundella kingdom. It has some interesting eighteenth century temples. The area is known for its diamond mines. The Majhganwa Diamond Mines nearby are open from 9 am to 1 pm, and closed on Sundays.

Kalanjar: 100 km, via Panna, on the Vindhya range. Built during the Gupta period, this fort was captured by the Chandella king Yashovarman in the mid tenth century. It twice withstood the siege of the Turkish invader Mahmud of Ghazni, in AD 1019 and 1022. The Nilakantheshvara temple, partly natural cave and partly man-made structure, is situated picturesquely with a magnificent view of the valley. The 24 ft. (7.3 m.) tall figure of Bhairava nearby was noted by Abul Fazal in the sixteenth century. The place is considered to be a holy *tirtha* (pilgrimage place) from the time of the *Mahabharata*.

Ajaygarh: 80 km; built on a high plateau. This fort town became a capital of the Chandellas in the declining days of the dynasty. There are temples built in the twelfth and thirteenth centuries within the fort. Getting there involves a climb.

Nachna: 100 km from Khajuraho via Panna, and about 4 km from

Ganj. The Parvati temple, built around AD 500, is a fine example of the Gupta style. The Chaturmukha Mahadeva temple enshrines a magnificent four-faced linga of about the eighth century. There are Jain and Vaishnavite antiquities in the compound. Worth visiting if one enjoys early Indian art, before the period of Khajuraho.

Bandhavgarh National Park: 240 km; in the heart of Vindhya mountain range in Shahdol district. Khajuraho is the nearest airport. This beautiful Park covers an area of 448 sq. km and has a variety of trees, plants and many wildlife species, including the white tiger. There are interesting archaeological remains, with stone sculptures of the Kalachuri period, contemporary with those of Khajuraho, and a fourteenth century fort. Best time to visit the Park is in winter. It is closed from July to October. It is advisable to spend at least two days here.

Orchha: 165 km; on the Betwa river, this sixteenth-seventeenth century Bundela capital has interesting palaces, temples, and cenotaphs of rulers. The mural paintings depicting secular and mythological themes on the palaces and temples are worth viewing. This site is 19 km south-east of Jhansi, and it would be convenient to visit it while travelling by road from Jhansi to Khajuraho or on the return journey.

Barwasagar: 22 km from Jhansi, on the main road to Khajuraho, is an exquisite temple dedicated to Jarai Mata (Mother goddess), built in the tenth century under the Pratihara dynasty. Its rectangular sanctum is typically associated with goddess temples. It has lovely sculptures, which one should not miss.

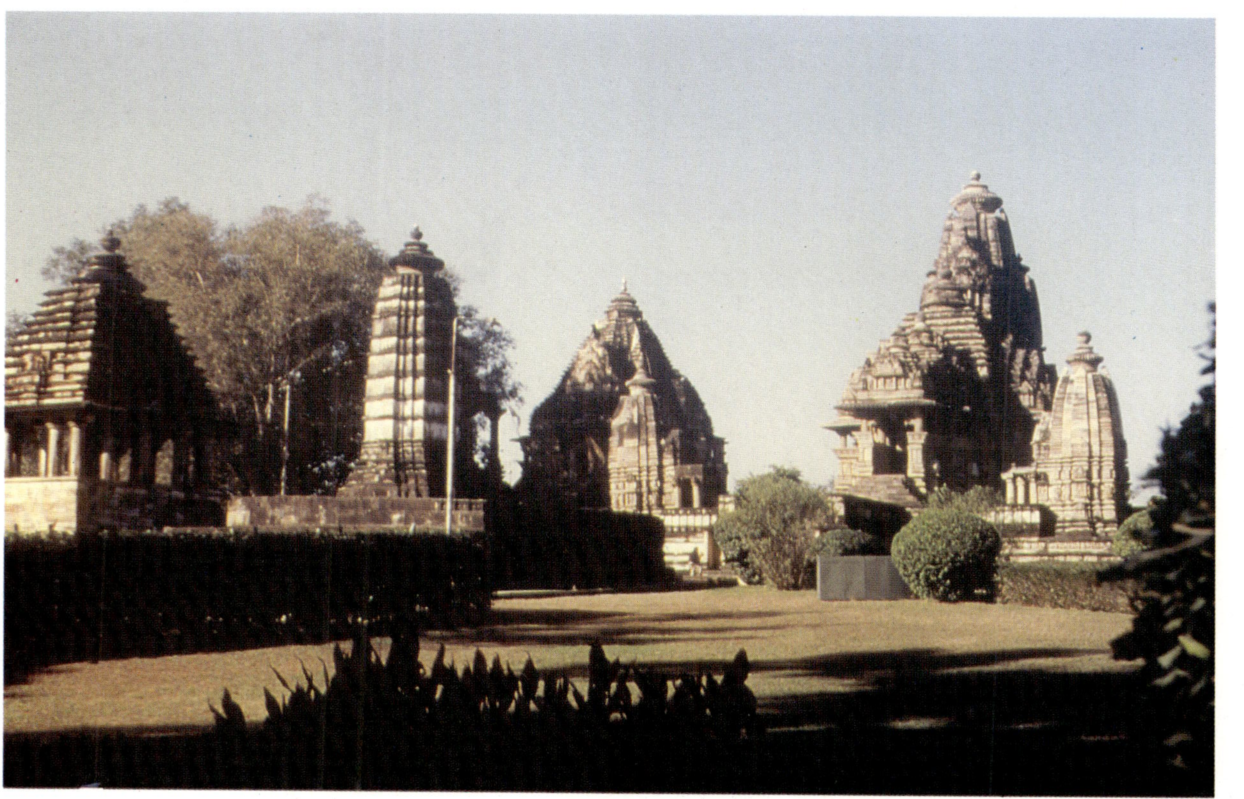

A. Temples in a group: Varaha, Devi, Matangeshvara and Lakshmana

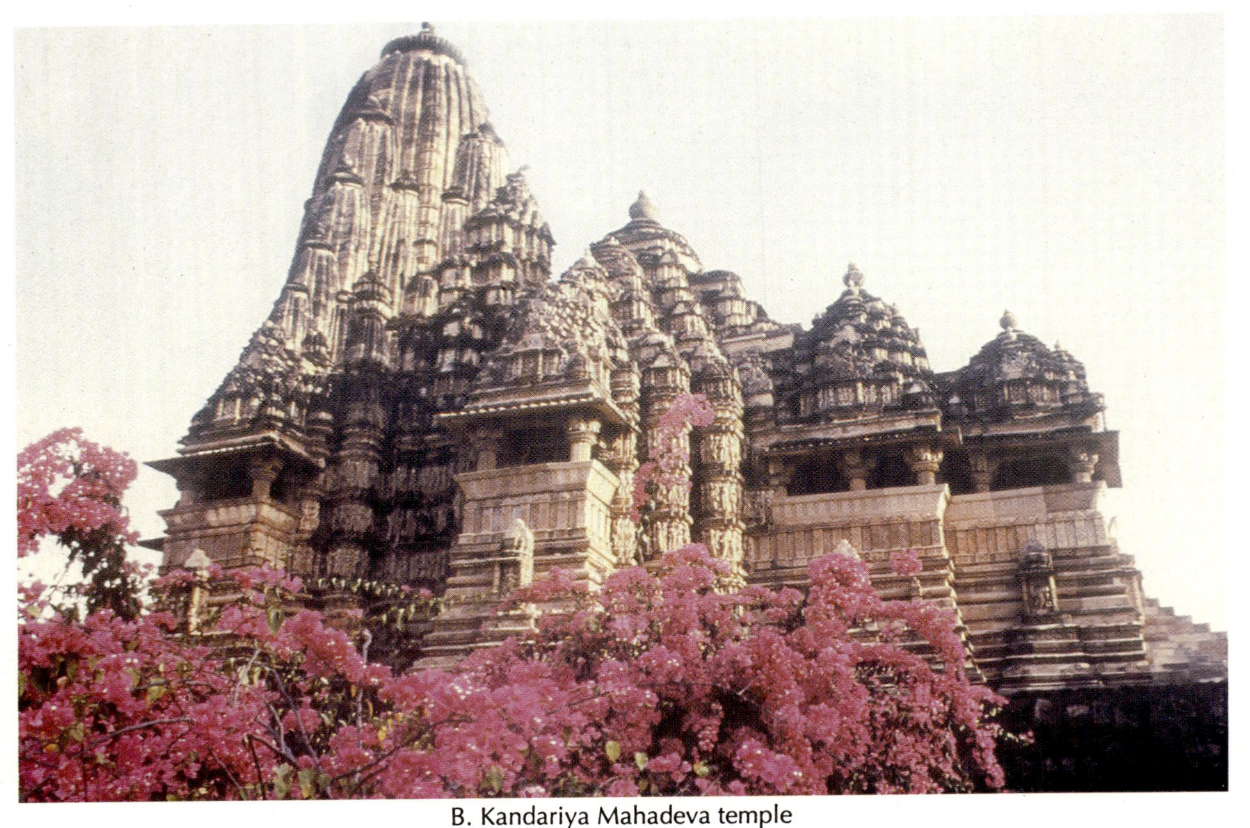

B. Kandariya Mahadeva temple

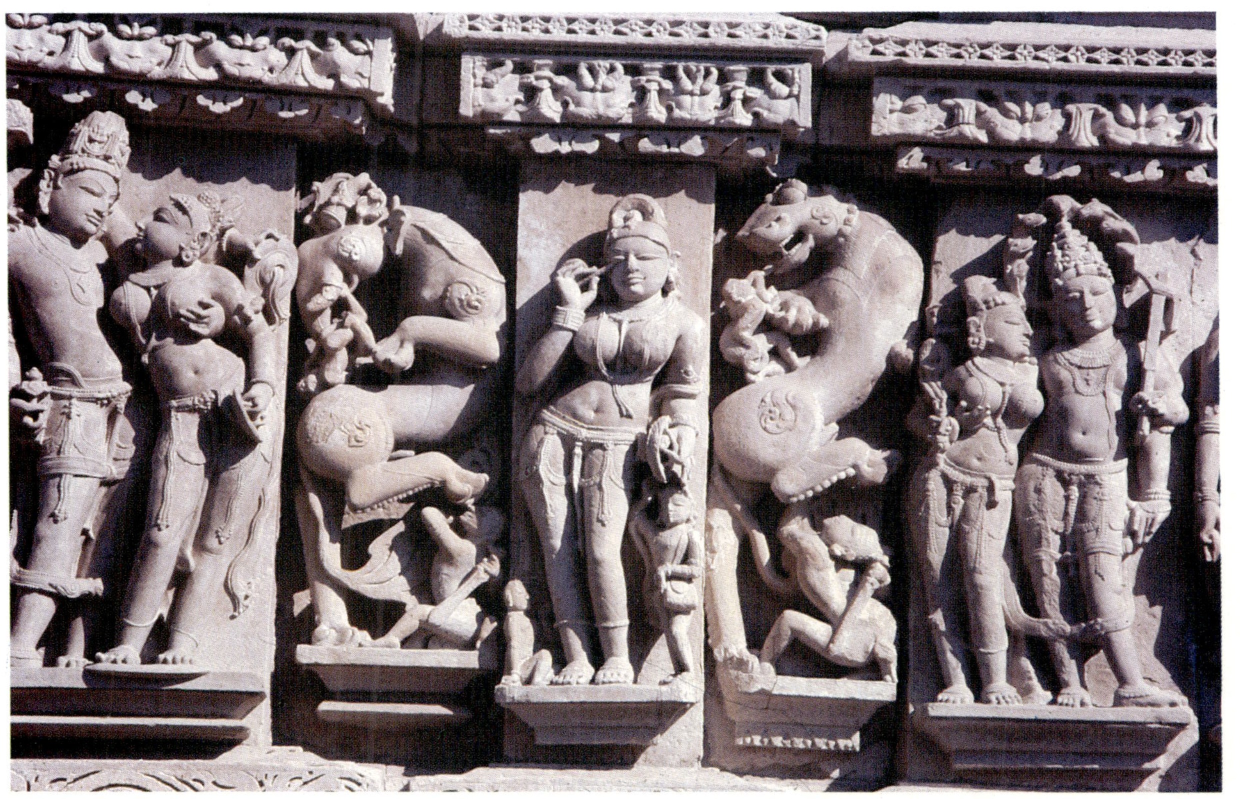

C. Sculptural imagery, Parshvanatha temple

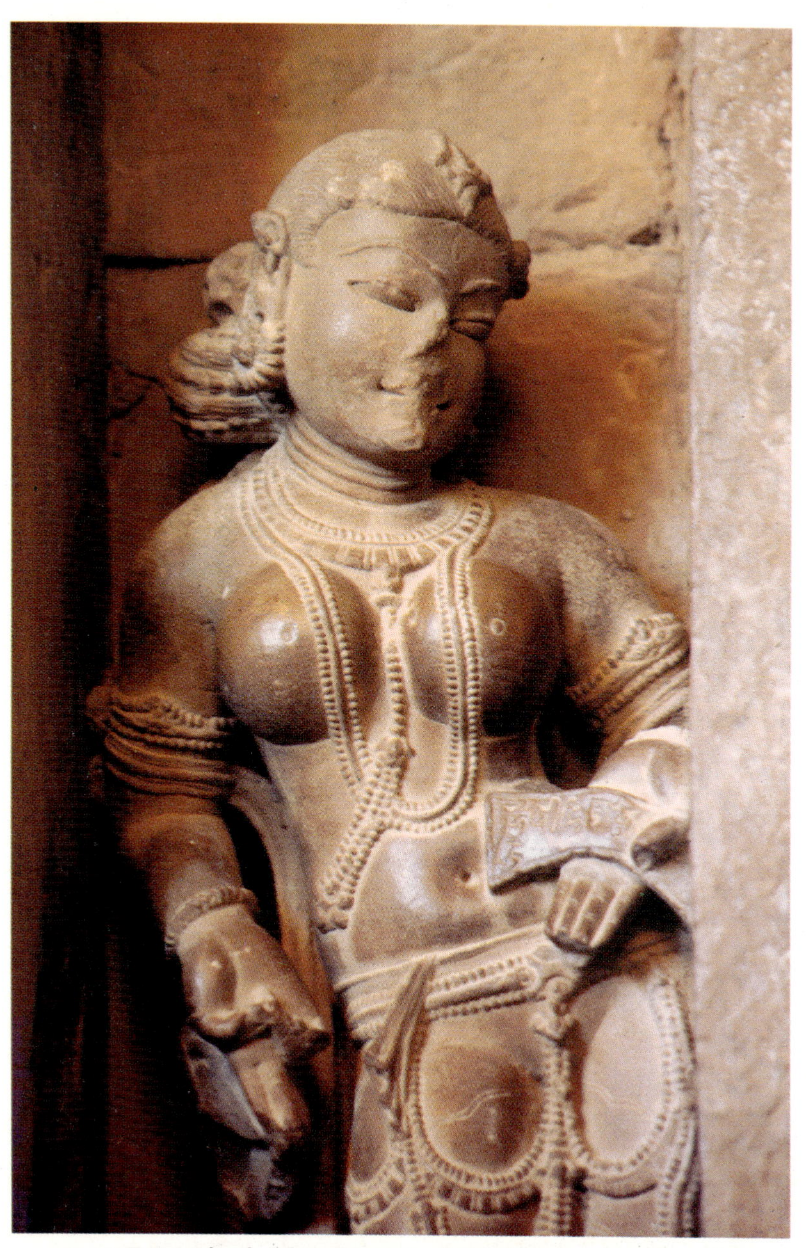

D. Maiden holding a manuscript, Lakshmana temple

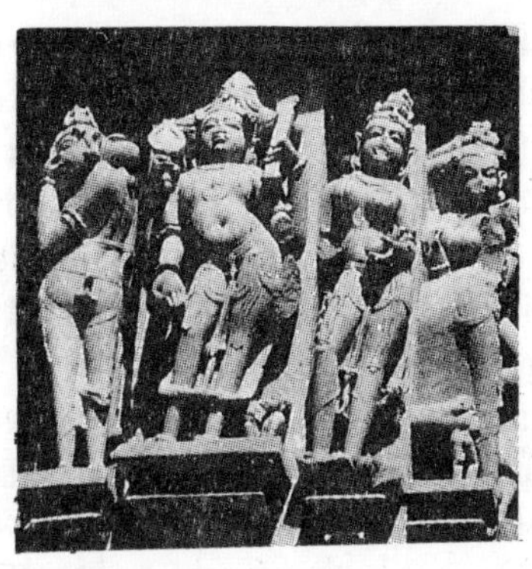

Appendix 1
Chronology of the Temples

1.	Chausath Yogini (Sixty-Four Goddesses)	*circa* AD 900
2.	Lalguan Mahadeva	*circa* AD 900–925
3.	Hanuman	Inscribed in the year equivalent to AD 922
4.	Brahma (originally dedicated to Vishnu)	*circa* AD 925
5.	Excavated brick temple complex	*circa* early tenth century AD
6.	Varaha (Boar incarnation of Vishnu)	*circa* AD 950, possibly commissioned by King Yashovarman
7.	Lakshmana (Vaikuntha form of Vishnu)	Built by King Yashovarman, *circa* AD 950, consecrated by his son Dhanga in AD 954
8.	Parshvanatha (Jain)	*circa* AD 950–970

9. Ghantai (Jain) — *circa* tenth century AD

10. Khakhra Matha (Vishnu) — *circa* tenth century AD

11. Vishvanatha (Shiva) — Inscribed VS 1056, equivalent to AD 999. Built by King Dhangadeva

12. Excavated Bijamandala (Vaidyanatha) temple — *circa* AD 1000

13. Matangeshvara (Shiva) — *circa* AD 1000

14. Devi Jagadamba (originally enshrined Vishnu) — *circa* AD 1000–1025

15. Chitragupta (Sun) — *circa* AD 1000–1025

16. Shantinatha (Jain) — *circa* AD 1027 or earlier in parts

17. Kandariya Mahadeva — *circa* AD 1030, possibly built by King Vidyadhara

18. Vamana (Dwarf incarnation of Vishnu) — *circa* AD 1050–1075

19. Adinatha (Jain) — *circa* AD 1075

20. Javari (Vishnu) — *circa* AD 1075–1100

21. Chaturbhuja (Vishnu) — *circa* AD 1110

22. Duladeva (Shiva) — *circa* AD 1130, possibly built by King Madanavarman

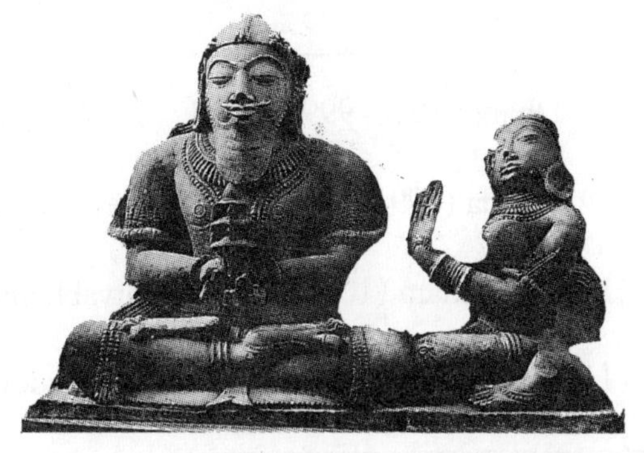

Appendix 2
Genealogy of the Chandella Royal Family

Chandratreya Muni

1. Nannuka (831–845)

2. Vakpati (845–865)

3. Jayashakti (865–885)   4. Vijayashakti

5. Rahila (885–905)

6. Harsha (905–925) = Kanchuka

7. Yashovarman (925–950) = Pushpa

8. Dhanga (950–999)   Krishnapa = Asarva

9. Ganda (999–1003)   Devalabdhi

10. Vidyadhara (1003–1035) = Satyabhama

11. Vijayapala (1035–1050) = Bhuvanadevi

12. Devavarman (1050–1060)   13. Kirtivarman (1060–1100)

14. Sallakshavarman (1100–1110)

15. Jayavarman (1110–1120)

16. Prithivivarman

17. Madanavarman (1128–1165) = Valhanadevi   Pratap
                             = Lakhamadevi
                             = Chandaladevi

Yashovarman II

18. Paramardideva (1165–1203)

19. Trailokyavarman (1203–1245)

20. Viravarman (1245–1285) = Kalyanadevi

21. Bhojavarman (1285–1288)

22. Hammiravarman (1288–1308)

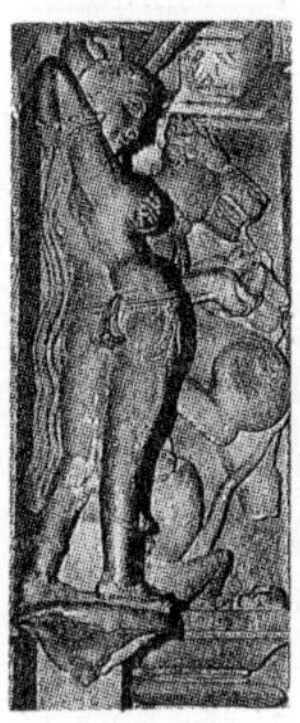

Practical Tips and Information

The best time to visit Khajuraho is between October and March. By the end of March it starts getting warmer and in May the temperature can rise upto 47° Celsius (117° Fahrenheit). By mid-September, the rains usually stop and the weather gradually becomes more pleasant.

Season:	Temperature	
	Maximum	Minimum
October–March	32°C	4°C
April–Sept	47°C	21°C
Rainfall during Monsoon	1120 mm. Mainly in July–August	

Hotel discounts are generally available during the off-season.

How to Reach Khajuraho:

Air: Daily Indian Airlines flights from Delhi, Agra, and Varanasi. Also connected to Bhopal, Indore, and Mumbai during the tourist season.
Jet Airways also operates flights during tourist season.

If you have to catch connecting flights from or to other cities, please do not keep your schedule too tight, because flights in this sector are sometimes delayed, particularly in winters, due to fog.

Rail: So far there is no direct railway connection to Khajuraho. Convenient Railway stations, from where you can get a taxi or bus to Khajuraho are:

1) Jhansi: 175 km away, on the Central Railway route—if you are travelling from Delhi, Chennai, or Mumbai. The Shatabdi Express leaves Delhi at 6.15 am and arrives in Jhansi at 10.40 am. There is a connecting deluxe bus from Jhansi to Khajuraho, and similarly, another for the return journey from Khajuraho, to meet the Shatabdi Express which leaves Jhansi for Agra and Delhi at 5.50 pm.

2) Satna: 117 km away, on the Central Railway route— if you are taking a train from Mumbai, Calcutta, Allahabad, or Varanasi.

Bus: Regular bus services from Jhansi, Satna, Mahoba, Chhatarpur, Harpalpur, Jabalpur, and Bhopal.
Jhansi to Khajuraho: About 4 1/2hours by A/C coach; 5–6 hours by ordinary bus.
Satna to Khajuraho: About 3 hours.

Road distance from major towns and cities:

Agra	395 km	Allahabad	285 km	Bhopal	372 km
Chhatarpur	49 km	Delhi	598 km	Gwalior	276 km
Harpalpur	102 km	Jabalpur	296 km	Jhansi	175 km
Mahoba	65 km	Mumbai	1250 km	Panna	44 km
Rewa	167 km	Satna	117 km	Varanasi	415 km

Local Transport:

Taxis and jeeps can be hired for local use and for excursions around Khajuraho from the MP Tourism office, Khajuraho Tours, and other Tour Operators or through your hotel. Cycle-rickshaws and auto-rickshaws are easily available for local

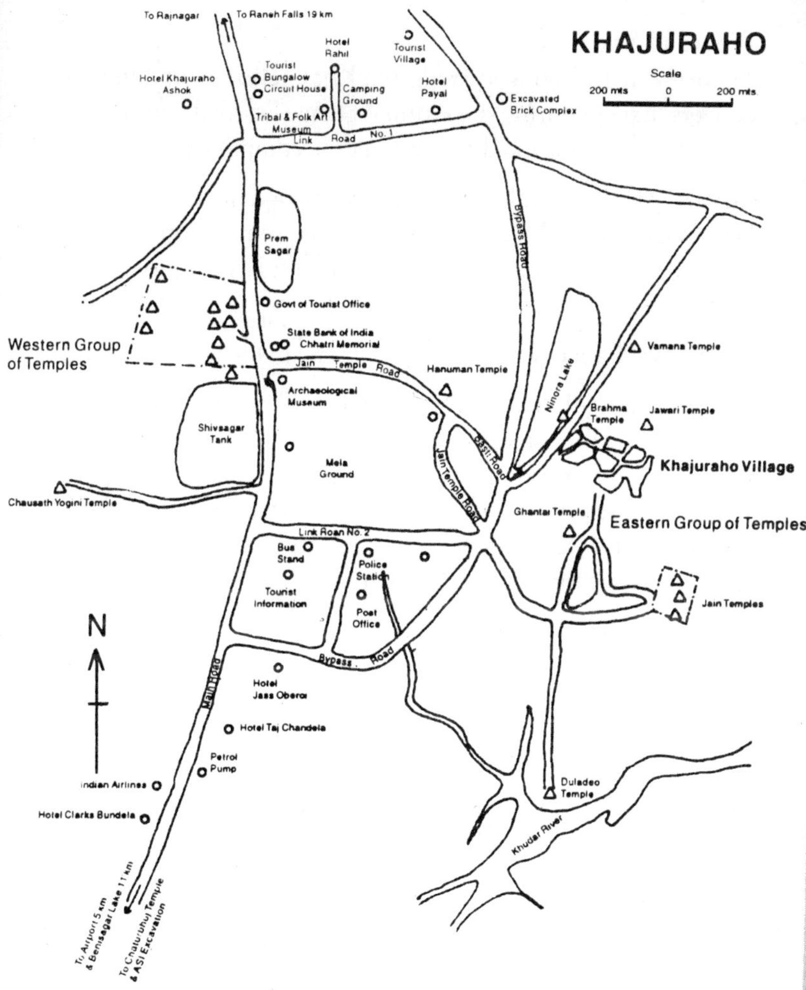

Fig. XIII. Khajuraho today

travel. Bicycles can be hired on a daily or hourly basis from a shop near the Museum.

The three temple-groups are not so far away from one another and can be reached in a few minutes by car or auto-rickshaws. To get a feel of the place you may travel by cycle-rickshaws or cycles, or walk, if you have time.

Where to Stay:
There are many hotels and lodges at Khajuraho to suit different budgets. Except during the Annual Dance Festival and similar occasions, it is not too difficult to get accommodation.

Luxury: Hotel Chandela (Management: Taj Group of Hotels); Hotel Jass Oberoi (Management: Oberoi Group); Hotel Clarks; Hotel Clarks Bundela; Holiday Inn; Hotel Khajuraho Ashok (ITDC).

Economy: Hotel Payal (MPSTDC); Hotel Jhankar (MPSTDC).

Budget: Hotel Rahil (MPSTDC); Tourist Bungalow (MPSTDC); Tourist Village Cottages (MPSTDC); Hotel Harmony; Hotel Surya; Jain Lodge; and many other places opposite the Western Group of Temples, and in the area behind the Museum. The Jain Dharamshala near the Eastern Group has Indian style accomodation at a very modest rate.

Where to eat:
Apart from the cafes attached to your hotel, which can be expensive in case of the Five Star hotels, there are modest restaurants:
Raja Café—Indian, Chinese, and Continental food. Nice open place below shady trees, facing the Western Group of Temples. It is managed by two Swiss ladies since 1978. Reasonable charges.
Madras Café—South Indian food and beverages, good *Dhosas*, *Idlis*, and coffee.
Delhi Restaurant—Serves Indian Thalis at lunch time, facing the Vishvanatha Temple of the Western Group; not expensive.

Tourist Offices:
1) Government of India Tourist Office,
   Opposite the Western Group of Temples, Khajuraho, Tel:
   42347/48
2) Tourist Office, MPSTDC,
   Tourist Bungalow Complex, Khajuraho, Tel: 42051

Tourist Guides—Speaking Hindi, English, French, Spanish, German, Italian, and Japanese. They can take you around the temples and shops in Khajuraho, and on site-seeing tours around Khajuraho. You may hire a guide for a full day or a half day through your Hotel, the Tourist Office or through Raja Café, where they generally sit during their free hours.

What to Wear:
Light woollens in the early mornings and late evenings during winter months. Please remember that you will have to remove footwear while entering the temples, in keeping with Indian religious custom. So it is advisable to wear easily removable footwear.

Medical Facilities:
There is a medical clinic near the bus stand.
There are medical shops in the Main Market and near the bus stand.

Banks:
State Bank of India, opposite the Western Group of Temples, Tel: 42373; and also at Hotel Chandela, Tel: 42173
Canara Bank, near the bus stand, Tel: 42071

Telephone: (STD Code 07686)
Khajuraho has STD facilities, connecting Indian centres, and ISD facilities connecting countries abroad. There are many telephone booths in shops near the Western Group of Temples. Fax facilities are also available in some of the shops.

Photographers:
Near the Western Group of Temples.

Shopping:
Handicrafts, textiles, and saris from Madhya Pradesh are sold at the State Government Emporium, Mriganayani, in the main market. Craft items, jewellery, curios, and brass and iron sculptures are available in the shops near the Western Group, and also near the Jain temples in the Eastern Group. Some of the village homes also have such articles for sale. Your rickshaw man can take you to such village shops. The major hotels have shopping arcades and book shops.

Festivals:
Khajuraho has two types of Festivals. A) Tourist festivals such as the week-long Dance Festival in March, organized by the Madhya Pradesh Government, when renowned Bharatanatyam, Odisi, and Kathak dancers are invited to perform against the backdrop of the illuminated temples of the Western Group. B) Village festivals: 1) Shivaratri in February or March. There is an interesting village fair for 10 days at this time, which is visited by thousands of people from nearby regions. 2) the Festival of Colours, Holi, in March. 3) the Mother Goddess Festival called Navaratri in October. 4) Divali (Festival of Lights), when village homes are decorated with rangoli (auspicious floor designs). There are other age-old festivals that the villagers still celebrate, during which you can see and hear village women singing their traditional songs.

Sound and Light Show:
This evening programme, introduced in December 1999 in the Western Group precincts, highlights historical and legendary aspects of Khajuraho.

Entry Fee to Temples and the ASI Museum:
A nominal entry fee is charged to visitors at the main gate of the Western Group, except on Fridays, when entry is free. This ticket is also valid for entry to the Archaeological Museum. The

Museum is open from 10 to 5 pm everyday except on Fridays. The monuments are open from sunrise to sunset every day.

Photography Permission:
Still photography at the monuments, without tripods, is permitted. For a video camera without a tripod there is a nominal fee. But for using a tripod, both for still photography as well as for video or film shooting, written permission is required from the Director General, Archaeological Survey of India, Janpath, New Delhi 110011. Photography at the Archaeological Museum requires a separate permission letter from the Archaeological Survey, Delhi office.

How to plan your visit of Khajuraho:

Western Group of temples	two to three hours
Eastern Group of temples	two to three hours
Chaturbhuja temple and, if possible, the newly excavated temple near Jatkari village	less than an hour, in the evening, as the temple faces west
The Archaeological Museum	about half an hour
Tribal and Folk Art Museum	about half an hour

If you have a second evening free, it would be worth the experience to sit on the south-west of the magnificent Kandariya Mahadeva temple and feel the rhythm of its mini-spires in the soft light of the setting sun.

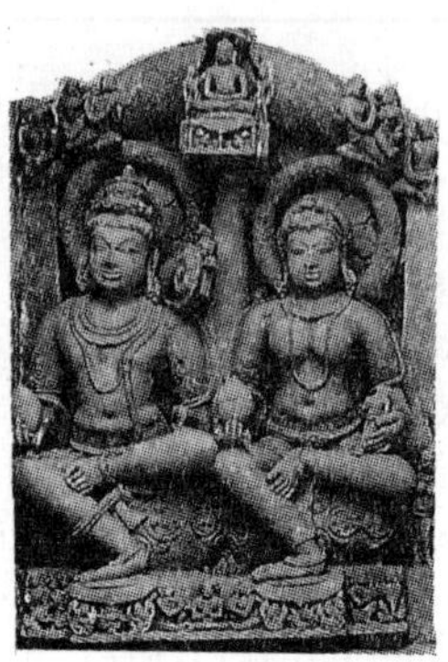

Glossary

abhaya-mudra	:	gesture of fearlessness in which the hand is raised palm outward with fingers pointing upward
Acharya	:	preceptor, religious teacher
Agni	:	god of Fire, regent of the south-east corner
alankara	:	ornament, decoration, embellishment
Andhakantaka	:	Shiva spearing the blind demon Andhaka
antarala	:	vestibule, passage between the hall and the sanctum
apsara	:	celestial maiden, motif in Indian art; cf. *surasundari*
Ardhanarishvara	:	'lord who is half woman', Shiva combined with his consort in a single body, male on the right side and female on the left
avarana-devata	:	divinities fencing or enclosing the principal icon
Bhairava	:	fearsome aspect of Shiva
Bhakti	:	religious devotion
Brahma	:	god of creation
chakra	:	discus or wheel, a weapon of Vishnu and other divinities; a subtle centre of energy in the human body
Chamunda	:	one of the Matrikas; goddess who destroys the demons Chanda and Munda
Chandra	:	Moon god

Chaturbhuja	:	four-armed; title of Vishnu
chatushpada	:	four-footed; (text) with four parts; applies to the four-footed Sadashiva image, and to Shaiva texts with four parts
dana	:	donation, gift
darshana	:	visual perception of the divinity
Devi	:	the Goddess
dhyana	:	meditation
Digambara	:	sky-clad or naked; one of the main Jain sects
Dikpalas	:	guardian deities of the eight directions of space. These are, starting from the east: Indra, Agni, Yama, Nirriti, Varuna, Vayu, Kubera, and Ishana.
Durga	:	warrior form of the Goddess, destroyer of demons, including the buffalo demon Mahisha
Dvarapala	:	door-guardian
gana	:	goblin; generally an attendant of Shiva
Ganesha	:	Lord of *ganas*; the elephant-faced god who removes obstacles
Ganga	:	the river goddess, stands on a *makara*. At the doorway of temples she is paired with the river goddess Yamuna
garbhagriha	:	'womb-house'; the sanctum of the temple which enshrines an icon or emblem of the divinity
Garuda	:	the mythic sun-bird; mount of Vishnu
Graha	:	planetary divinity. In mythology there are nine planets; collectively these are called Nava-Grahas.
Guru	:	religious teacher, preceptor
Hanuman	:	Monkey god
Hari-Hara	:	composite form in which Vishnu is on the left, Shiva on the right
Hayagriva	:	horse-headed incarnation of Vishnu who rescues the Vedas
jagati	:	platform on which the temple is built
jangha	:	literally, thigh; in temple architecture central portion of the wall
jata	:	matted locks of hair
jata-mukuta	:	head-gear or crown of matted locks of hair
Jina	:	victorious; Jain Tirthankara. There are 24 Jinas.
Kailasa	:	the mountain abode of Shiva in the Himalayas; temples are compared in inscriptions to mounts Kailasa and Meru

kama	:	desire, love; one of the four aims of life
Kamasutra	:	fourth century text on technicalities of sex, written by Vatsyayana
Kapalika	:	skull-bearer; member of an extreme Tantric sect
kapili	:	juncture-wall connecting the sanctum and the hall
Karttikeya	:	son of Shiva; commander of the army of gods; also portrayed as a teacher with a book at Khajuraho
kharjura	:	date-palm tree; scorpion. The ancient name of Khajuraho (Kharjura-vahaka) is derived from this word.
kirita-mukuta	:	conical crown worn by Vishnu and Surya
kirtimukha	:	'face of glory', protective motif used in decoration
Krishna	:	cowherd god, the eighth incarnation of Vishnu
Krishna-lila	:	Krishna's childhood sports
Kshetrapala	:	guardian of the field or land
Kubera	:	lord of wealth, king of Yakshas; Dikpala of the north direction
Kundalini	:	energy or *shakti* believed to lie dormant in each individual at the base of the spine, which, when awakened and brought by the aspirant to the upper Sahasrara *chakra*, leads to the state of highest bliss
Kurma	:	Tortoise incarnation of Vishnu
Lakshmi	:	goddess of wealth and beauty, wife of Vishnu
lila-murtis	:	'playful' manifestations of Shiva, such as the Cosmic Dancer and the Bridegroom. These are not placed in the centre of the sanctum, but in the surrounding niches of the sanctum.
linga	:	aniconic emblem of Shiva, installed in the sanctum and worshipped; conceived as the cosmic axis in a Chandella inscription.
mahamandapa	:	large columnar hall between the *mandapa* and *antarala*
Mahesha	:	'the great lord', manifest (*vyakta*) aspect of Shiva
Mahishasura-mardini	:	Goddess Durga who destroys Mahishasura, the buffalo demon
makara	:	mythic aquatic creature; auspicious motif; mount of Varuna and the river goddess Ganga
mandala	:	literally, a circle; a circular diagram; geometric design of cosmic order

mandapa	:	hall
mangala	:	auspicious, lucky
mantra	:	mystical formula sacred to a deity; incantation
Matrikas	:	Divine Mothers, often standardized into a group of seven. Their standard sequence in worship: Brahmani, Maheshvari, Kaumari, Vaishnavi, Varahi, Aindri, and Chamunda
Matsya	:	Fish incarnation of Vishnu
Meru	:	mythical mountain considered to be the centre of the world
mithuna	:	pair, couple; an auspicious motif in Indian art
mukhamandapa	:	porch, front hall
mukuta	:	crown
murti	:	icon, image
naga	:	snake; *nagini* is the female
Nagara	:	the Northern Indian style of temple architecture
Nandi	:	Shiva's bull
Narasimha	:	Man-Lion incarnation of Vishnu
narathara	:	sculptured row on the plinth of the temple
Narayana	:	Vishnu as master of Yoga, associated with ascetics
Natesha	:	Shiva as the lord of dance
Nava-Grahas	:	nine planetary divinities, including the Sun and Moon
nayika	:	heroine of a literary composition
nirandhara	:	without an ambulatory around the sanctum
pada	:	foot; (of a text) quarter part
padmasana	:	lotus posture of sitting during worship and meditation, in which both legs are crossed
Pancharatra	:	Tantric Vaishnavite religious system. Its Kashmir school worships the many-headed Vishnu-Vaikuntha, as in Khajuraho's Lakshmana temple
panchayatana	:	five-shrined complex; a temple with four subsidiary shrines
Parvati	:	wife of Shiva; another name of Uma
pradakshina	:	circumambulation; walking in a clock-wise direction keeping the object of worship on the right
Prithivi	:	Earth goddess
puja	:	worship
Purana	:	religious text of Hindu myths, legends; there are 18 Puranas
Puranic	:	pertaining to the Puranas

Purta-dharma	:	religious practice which involves charitable works, gifts to Brahmins, building of temples and tanks
Sadashiva	:	a form of Shiva intermediate between unmanifest Supreme Being and manifest Mahesha
samabhanga	:	standing posture in which the figure is equipoised, with weight equally distributed on both the feet
sandhara	:	with an ambulatory around the sanctum
sandhya bhasha	:	intentional double-meaning language, used by the Tantric followers and mystics to conceal their doctrines from the non-initiated
Sarasvati	:	goddess of learning and wisdom
Shaivite	:	believer in Shiva as the Supreme Deity
Shakta	:	worshipper of the feminine creative force
Shakti	:	energy; the feminine creative force; personification of the energy of a god
shalabhanjika	:	woman-and-tree motif
shikhara	:	in North Indian architecture, the spire over the *garbhagriha* or sanctum
Shilpashastra	:	treatise on the rules of sculpture, architecture, and allied arts; cf. Vastushastra
Shiva	:	one of the principal Hindu gods, associated with the Destruction or Reabsorbtion of the universe. In the Shaivite system, he is the Supreme Creator, Protector, and Destroyer
shubha	:	auspicious
surasundari	:	celestial maiden; a motif in temple art; cf. *apsara*
Surya	:	Sun god
Sutradhara	:	holder of *sutra* or thread, cord. In Chandella inscriptions the word is also used for the master-architect
Tantric	:	referring to a class of non-Vedic texts called Tantra that advocated spiritual discipline and magic rituals for the attainment of union with the Supreme Being, and which influenced Hinduism, Buddhism, and Jainism in the medieval period
tirtha	:	pilgrimage centre
Tirthankara	:	sanctified saint of Jainism, there are 24 Tirthankaras
torana	:	gateway
tribhanga	:	standing posture with three bends
Tripurantaka	:	manifestation of Shiva destroying the three demon cities

trishula	:	trident
Uma	:	wife of Shiva, another name of Parvati
Uma-Maheshvara	:	Uma with Maheshvara (Shiva)
vahana	:	mount
Vaikuntha	:	composite form of Vishnu with faces of a Lion, a Man, a Boar, and a Horse. Khajuraho has a major temple (Lakshmana) enshrining an image of Vaikuntha.
Vamana	:	Dwarf incarnation of Vishnu
varada mudra	:	gesture of bestowing a boon in which the palm is held downward facing the devotee
Varaha	:	Boar incarnation of Vishnu, represented in Khajuraho as 1) cosmic animal (Yajna-Varaha), and 2) as half-man half-animal (Nri-Varaha)
Varuna	:	god of the ocean; Dikpala of the west direction
Vastushastra	:	treatise on the rules of architecture, sculpture, and allied arts
Vasus	:	group of eight semi-divine bull-headed beings regarded as atmospheric powers, believed to be associated with wealth and splendour. In the Khajuraho temples, the Vasus are placed in the eight directions, above the images of the Dikpalas
Vedas	:	ancient scriptural corpus of sacred knowledge; the four collected works
vedibandha	:	basal wall mouldings
vidyadhara	:	semi-divine being flying in the air
vina	:	stringed musical instrument
Vishnu	:	one of the principal Hindu gods, associated with protection. In the Vaishnavite system, he is the Supreme Creator, Protector, and Destroyer
vyala	:	griffin; composite fantastic creature; motif in art
yajna	:	oblation; sacrificial rite
Yaksha	:	(female-Yakshi) nature divinity, associated with earth, water, and vegetation. In Jainism Yakshas and Yakshis are attendants of each of the 24 Tirthankaras.
Yamuna	:	river goddess, stands on a tortoise
Yantra	:	geometric diagram; abstract symbol of divinity used as a tool for meditation
Yoga	:	discipline involving psycho-physical practices

		with the aim of realizing concentration of the mind and union with the universal consciousness
yogasana	:	yogic posture; cf. *padmasana*
Yogin	:	one who practises Yoga
Yoginis	:	female divinities who are companions or manifestations of the Great Goddess. Khajuraho has a specially built sanctuary for the 64 Yoginis.

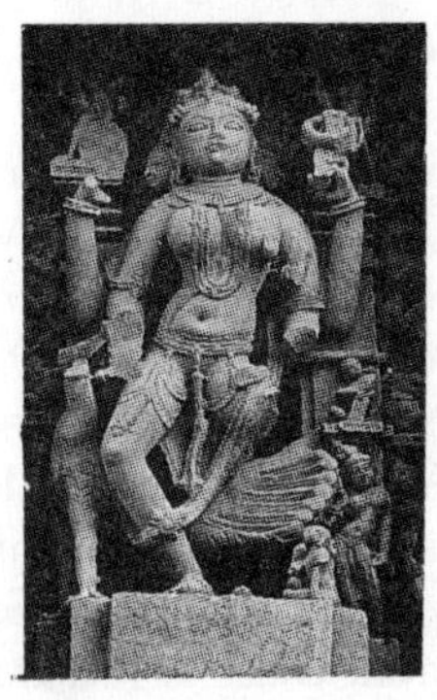

Further Reading

Awasthi, R.: *Khajuraho ki Deva Pratimayen* (Hindi), Oriental Publishing House, Agra 1967.

Banerjea, J.N.: *The Development of Hindu Iconography*, second edition, University of Calcutta, Calcutta 1956.

————: *Pauranic and Tantric Religion*, Calcutta University Press, Calcutta 1966.

Chakravarty, K.K., M.N. Tiwari, and Kamal Giri (eds): *Khajuraho in Perspective*, Department of State Archaeology and Museums, Bhopal 1994.

Cunningham, Alexander: *Archaeological Survey of India Reports*, Vols. II, VII, X, XXI, Simla-Calcutta 1864–85.

Dehejia, Vidya: *Yogini Cult and Temples, A Tantric Tradition*, National Museum, New Delhi 1986.

Desai, Devangana: *Erotic Sculpture of India—A Socio-Cultural Study*, first published Tata McGraw Hill, New Delhi 1975; second revised edition, Munshiram Manoharlal, New Delhi 1985.

————: 'Placement and Significance of Erotic Sculptures at Khajuraho', in Michael W. Meister, ed. *Discourses on Siva*, University of Pennsylvania Press, Philadelphia 1984.

————: 'Shades of Eroticism in Temple Art', in Saryu Doshi, ed. *Symbols and Manifestations in Indian Art*, Marg Publications, Bombay 1984.

————: *The Religious Imagery of Khajuraho*, Franco-Indian Research, Mumbai 1996.

————: 'Significance of the New Find at Khajuraho: Gahapati Kokkala's Vaidyanatha Temple?' in *Marg* magazine, Vol. 51, No. 3, 2000.

Desai, Vishakha and Darielle Mason: *Gods, Gaurdians, and Lovers, Temple Sculptures From Northern India* AD 700–1200, Asia Society, New York, and Mapin Publishers, Ahmedabad 1993.

Deva, Krishna: *Khajuraho*, ASI, first edition 1965; Reprint, New Delhi 1996.

————: *Khajuraho*, Brijbasi Printers, New Delhi 1987.

————: *Temples of Khajuraho*, two volumes, ASI, New Delhi 1990.

Deva, Krisna and B.S. Nayal: *Guide to Khajuraho Museum*, ASI, New Delhi 1980.

Dhama, B.L.: *A Guide to Khajuraho*, Chhatarpur State, Bombay 1927.

Dikshit, R.K.: *The Candellas of Jejakabhukti*, Abhinav Publications, New Delhi 1977.

Eliade, Mircea: *Yoga: Immortality and Freedom*, Bollingen Series, LVI, New York 1958.

Imperial Gazetteer of India, Central India, first edition 1908, reprint, New Delhi 1989.

Khanna, Madhu: *Yantra*, Thames and Hudson, London 1979.

Kramrisch, Stella: *The Hindu Temple*, two volumes, 1946, reprint by Motilal Banarsidass 1976.

Meister, Michael: 'Juncture and Conjunction: Punning and Temple Architecture', *Artibus Asiae*, XLI, 1979.

Michell, George: *The Hindu Temple, An Introduction to its Meanings and Forms*, B.I. Publishers, Bombay 1977.

Mitra, S.K.: *The Early Rulers of Khajuraho*, Motilal Banarsidass, second revised edition, Delhi 1977.

Pal, Pratapaditya: *Hindu Religion and Iconology*, Vichitra Press, Los Angeles 1981.

Prakash, Vidya: *Khajuraho, A Study in the Cultural Conditions of Chandella Society*, Taraporevalas, Bombay 1967.

Punja, Shobita: *Khajuraho and Its Historic Surroundings*, Guide Book Company, 1995.

Rao, T.A. Gopinatha: *Elements of Hindu Iconography*, in two volumes, 1916, Reprint, Indological Book House, New Delhi 1971.

Thapar, Romila: *Ancient Indian Social History*, Orient Longman, New Delhi 1978.

Tiwari, Maruti Nandan: *Khajuraho ka Jaina Puratattva*, (Hindi), Sahu Shanti Prasad Jain Kala Sangrahalaya, Khajuraho 1987;

————: *Guide to Sahu Shantiprasad Jain Kala Sangrahalaya, Khajuraho*, (Hindi), Shri Digambar Jain Atishaya Kshetra Khajuraho Prabandha Samiti, Khajuraho 1992.

Zannas, Eliky, and J. Auboyer: *Khajuraho*, Mouton and Company, The Hague, 1960.

Zimmer, Heinrich: *Myths and Symbols in Indian Art and Civilization*, 1946, Bollingen Reprint, 1974.